W9-CEL-236

FLASH FORWARD MATH

Written by **Shannon Keeley**

Illustrations by **Mark Stephens**

Flash Kids
A Division of Barnes & Noble
122 Fifth Ave
New York, NY 10011

ISBN: 978-1-4114-2798-3

Please submit all inquiries to FlashKids@bn.com

Printed and bound in the United States

1 3 5 7 9 10 8 6 4 2

Prime Climb

Find all the rocks with prime numbers and circle them.
There are 24 prime numbers on the wall in total.

A *prime number* is a number that has only two factors—1 and the number itself. For example, 3 is a prime number because its only factors are 1 and 3.

Negative Numbers

Negative numbers are numbers less than zero. Use the number line to help solve these problems with negative numbers.

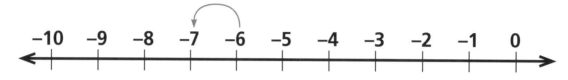

Solve the problems by adding the negative numbers together. Find the first negative number on the number line. Move left to add the second negative number. The first one is done for you.

1. −6 + −1 = ___-7___

2. −1 + −2 = _____

3. −5 + −2 = _____

4. −4 + −4 = _____

5. −5 + −4 = _____

6. −3 + −3 = _____

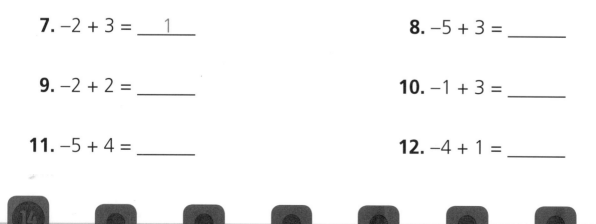

Solve the problems by finding the negative number on the number line. Move right to add the positive number. Don't forget to count the zero as you move to the right. The first one is done for you.

7. −2 + 3 = ___1___

8. −5 + 3 = _____

9. −2 + 2 = _____

10. −1 + 3 = _____

11. −5 + 4 = _____

12. −4 + 1 = _____

Crack the Code

Find the missing number in each equation.
Use the code to answer the joke.

1.
$$\begin{array}{r} 3,415 \\ + \boxed{} \\ \hline 6,252 \end{array}$$
Z

2.
$$\begin{array}{r} \boxed{} \\ - 1,522 \\ \hline 492 \end{array}$$
S

3.
$$\begin{array}{r} 429 \\ - \boxed{} \\ \hline 74 \end{array}$$
L

4.
$$\begin{array}{r} 138 \\ + \boxed{} \\ \hline 641 \end{array}$$
U

5.
$$\begin{array}{r} 1,098 \\ + \boxed{} \\ \hline 1,321 \end{array}$$
O

6.
$$\begin{array}{r} \boxed{} \\ - 74 \\ \hline 228 \end{array}$$
Z

7.
$$\begin{array}{r} 202 \\ - \boxed{} \\ \hline 48 \end{array}$$
C

8.
$$\begin{array}{r} 302 \\ - \boxed{} \\ \hline 52 \end{array}$$
B

9.
$$\begin{array}{r} \boxed{} \\ + 299 \\ \hline 1,329 \end{array}$$
O

10.
$$\begin{array}{r} 109 \\ + \boxed{} \\ \hline 1,737 \end{array}$$
H

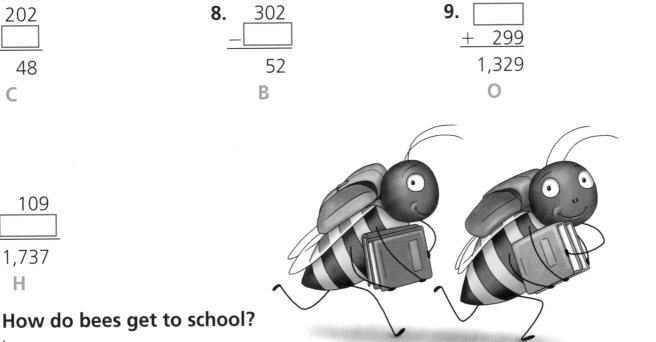

How do bees get to school?

In a

$\overline{}$ $\overline{}$ $\overline{}$ $\overline{}$ $\overline{}$ $\overline{}$ $\overline{}$ $\overline{}$ $\overline{}$ $\overline{}$
2,014   154   1,628   1,030   223   355   250   503   2837   302

First Aid

Solve the equation inside the parentheses first as you do each equation.

> Parentheses tell us which problem to do first.
>
> $\overset{7}{\overbrace{(10 - 3)}} + 2 = 9$ $10 - \overset{5}{\overbrace{(3 + 2)}} = 5$

1. $(8 - 4) - 2 =$ _____

2. $10 - (9 - 3) =$ _____

3. $(5 - 0) - 1 =$ _____

4. $8 - (3 + 3) =$ _____

5. $(12 - 2) + 3 =$ _____

6. $14 - (5 + 6) =$ _____

7. $9 - (4 + 5) =$ _____

8. $(15 - 4) + 3 =$ _____

9. $7 + (10 - 4) =$ _____

10. $(6 - 2) + 8 =$ _____

11. $12 - (9 - 2) =$ _____

12. $5 + (12 - 3) =$ _____

Pizza Problems

Solve each problem.

1. So far this year the pizza place has delivered 3,208 pepperoni pizzas, 2,455 sausage pizzas, and 4,856 cheese pizzas. They have a goal to deliver 12,000 pizzas before the end of the year. How many more pizzas do they need to deliver to meet their goal?

_____

2. The "Ten-Topping Super Pizza" has 18 pepperoni pieces, 12 mushrooms, 8 red bell peppers, 8 green bell peppers, 10 meatballs, 15 sausage pieces, 9 tomatoes, 22 pineapple chunks, 13 onion pieces, and 7 olives. How many toppings are on the pizza altogether?

_____

3. This month, the pizza place made a total of 1,031 pizzas. Of those pizzas, 644 were delivered to people's homes and 287 pizzas were picked up by the customers. The rest of the pizzas were eaten at the pizza place. How many pizzas were eaten at the pizza place?

_____

4. On Saturday the pizza place sold 118 pizzas at lunchtime and 178 at dinnertime. On Sunday the pizza place sold 74 pizzas at lunch and 204 pizzas at dinner. On which day did the pizza place sell the most pizzas in all?

_____

Designer Decimals

Add or subtract the decimals.

1.   4.35
    + 3.86

2.   25.05
    − 18.5

3.   0.75
    − 0.28

4. $215.89
    + $26.99

5.   12.63
    − 5.09

6.   22.01
    + 176.99

7. $0.89
   + $10.09

8. $307.49
    − $112.99

9.   604.33
    − 603.43

10. 0.0.
    + 2.99

11.   500.9
    + 90.05

12. 641.7
   − 614.07

Down and Across Decimals

Solve each problem and write the answer in the cross-number puzzle.
Use one box for a decimal point.

Across

3. 760.4 − 558.01 = _____

6. 0.88 + 4.4 = _____

8. 425.6 + 452.6 = _____

9. 300 − 100.3 = _____

10. 346.01 + 371 = _____

Down

1. 571.52 − 346 = _____

2. 637.02 − 109.82 = _____

4. 117.07 + 171.7 = _____

5. 242.69 + 146.03 = _____

7. 158.09 − 56.93 = _____

Fruity Fractions

Add or subtract the fractions.

1. $\dfrac{7}{8} - \dfrac{5}{8} = $ —

2. $\dfrac{2}{5} + \dfrac{1}{5} = $ —

3. $\dfrac{1}{3} + \dfrac{1}{3} = $ —

4. $\dfrac{7}{9} + \dfrac{2}{9} = $ —

5. $\dfrac{5}{7} - \dfrac{2}{7} = $ —

6. $\dfrac{9}{10} - \dfrac{8}{10} = $ —

7. $\dfrac{8}{9} - \dfrac{5}{9} = $ —

8. $\dfrac{3}{8} + \dfrac{1}{8} = $ —

9. $\dfrac{2}{5} + \dfrac{2}{5} = $ —

10. $\dfrac{3}{7} + \dfrac{1}{7} = $ —

11. $\dfrac{3}{10} + \dfrac{3}{10} = $ —

12. $\dfrac{4}{5} - \dfrac{2}{5} = $ —

Candy Count

Count the number of each type of candy and write the fraction below.
Then add or subtract. The first one is done for you.

1.  $+$ $=$ $\dfrac{3}{10}$

$\dfrac{2}{10}$ $+$ $\dfrac{1}{10}$ $=$

2.  $-$ $=$ ____

3.  $+$ $=$ ____

4. $+$ $=$ ____

5. $-$ $=$ ____

6. $-$ $=$ ____

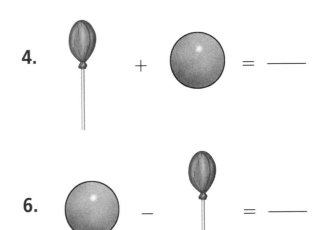

Stop, Drop, and Drill

Stop and read each problem carefully. Add or subtract to complete the drill.

1. $4.35 - 2.4 =$ _____

2. $\dfrac{3}{8} + \dfrac{1}{8} =$ —

3. $6.1 - (3.02 + 2) =$ _____

4. $12{,}364 + 8{,}285 =$ _____

5. $\dfrac{5}{6} - \left(\dfrac{4}{6} - \dfrac{1}{6}\right) =$ —

6. $2{,}304 + 23.04 =$ _____

7. $\$0.75 + \$0.99 =$ _____

8. $425.07 - 230.5 =$ _____

9. $(134.2 - 13.42) - 1.34 =$ _____

10. $5 - 2.09 =$ _____

11. $\$20.00 - \$8.75 =$ _____

12. $\dfrac{7}{9} - \left(\dfrac{2}{9} + \dfrac{2}{9}\right) =$ —

The Pie Guy

Solve each problem.

1. The Pie Guy cut an apple pie into 8 equal slices. One customer bought 2 slices and then another bought 3. What fraction of the pie is left?

2. A slice of pie costs $1.25. Sara bought three slices of pie and paid for them with a twenty-dollar bill. How much change did she get back?

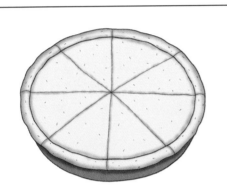

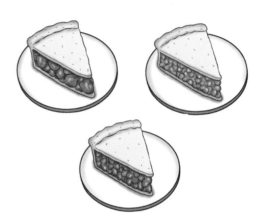

3. The Pie Guy baked 4 berry pies at the beginning of the day. He cut each pie into 6 slices. At the end of the day, he still had $\frac{1}{6}$ of the strawberry pie, $\frac{1}{6}$ of the blueberry pie, $\frac{1}{3}$ of the blackberry pie, and $\frac{1}{6}$ of the raspberry pie. If the Pie Guy put all the pieces of berry pie together in one pie pan, what fraction of a pie would he have?

4. The pie box can hold only 20 ounces without breaking. The Pie Guy just baked a cherry pie that has 12.05 ounces of cherry filling. The piecrust weighs 5.8 ounces and the whipped cream weighs 3 ounces. Can the box hold the pie without breaking?

Roosevelt School Raffle

The students at Roosevelt School sold raffle tickets for $1.25 each to raise money. Use the table to answer the questions.

Grade	Number of Raffle Tickets Sold	Money Raised
1	107	$133.75
2	214	$267.50
3	301	$376.25
4	149	$186.25
5	208	$260.00
6	265	$331.25

1. If you compare the total number of tickets sold for grades 1–3 and the total number sold for grades 4–6, which group sold more tickets?

_____

2. How much more money did grade 3 raise than grade 2?

_____

3. If you round the number of tickets sold to the nearest hundred, how many grade levels would round to 200?

_____

4. Which grade's earnings can you combine with grade 5's to equal $393.75?

_____

5. Round the number of raffle tickets each grade sold to the nearest hundred, and add all the rounded numbers together. Then add up the exact number of tickets sold altogether. What is the difference between the rounded total and the exact total?

_____

6. How much did the students in all six grades raise altogether? _____

Patty's Pet Shop

The tally chart shows how many of each kind of pet Patty has in her shop. Use the chart to answer the questions below.

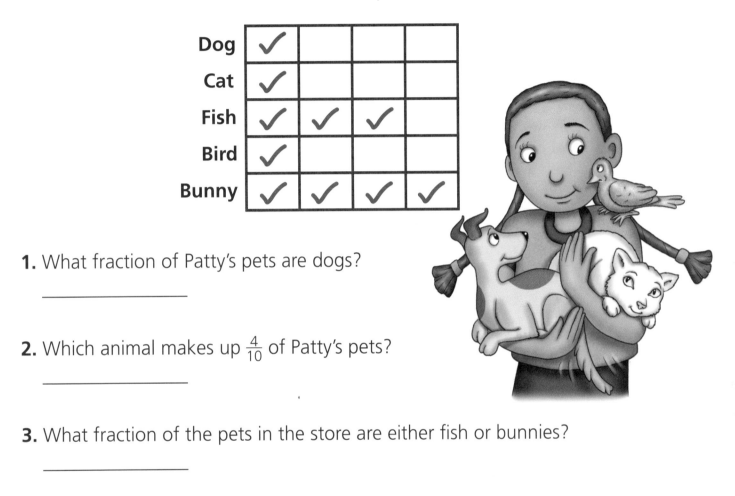

Dog	✓			
Cat	✓			
Fish	✓	✓	✓	
Bird	✓			
Bunny	✓	✓	✓	✓

1. What fraction of Patty's pets are dogs?

_____

2. Which animal makes up $\frac{4}{10}$ of Patty's pets?

_____

3. What fraction of the pets in the store are either fish or bunnies?

_____

4. Which three animals added together make up $\frac{3}{10}$ of the pets in the store?

_____ _____ _____

5. A customer bought all of the fish in the pet shop. What fraction of the pets are still there? _____

6. Patty put the dog, the cat, and the bunnies in the bath. What fraction of the pets are in the bath? _____

Bulls-Eye Multiply

Multiply to solve each problem. Remember to regroup.

1. 38
× 4

2. 245
× 5

3. 57
× 8

4. 309
× 3

5. 2,816
× 2

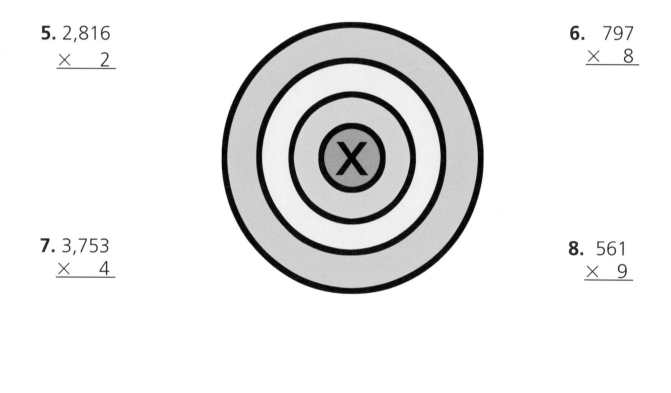

6. 797
× 8

7. 3,753
× 4

8. 561
× 9

9. 10,648
× 6

10. 1,504
× 7

11. 99
× 8

12. 7,040
× 5

Find the Four

Multiply to solve each problem. Circle the row with four equal answers. The row can go across, down, or diagonally. The first problem is done for you.

1. $\begin{array}{r} \scriptstyle 1 \\ 17 \\ \times\ 12 \\ \hline \scriptstyle 1\ 34 \\ \times 17 \\ \hline 204 \end{array}$	**2.** $\begin{array}{r} 83 \\ \times\ 30 \\ \hline \end{array}$	**3.** $\begin{array}{r} 132 \\ \times\ 22 \\ \hline \end{array}$	**4.** $\begin{array}{r} 484 \\ \times\ 6 \\ \hline \end{array}$
5. $\begin{array}{r} 12 \\ \times\ 20 \\ \hline \end{array}$	**6.** $\begin{array}{r} 66 \\ \times\ 44 \\ \hline \end{array}$	**7.** $\begin{array}{r} 242 \\ \times\ 12 \\ \hline \end{array}$	**8.** $\begin{array}{r} 58 \\ \times\ 5 \\ \hline \end{array}$
9. $\begin{array}{r} 264 \\ \times\ 11 \\ \hline \end{array}$	**10.** $\begin{array}{r} 121 \\ \times\ 24 \\ \hline \end{array}$	**11.** $\begin{array}{r} 147 \\ \times\ 20 \\ \hline \end{array}$	**12.** $\begin{array}{r} 88 \\ \times\ 33 \\ \hline \end{array}$
13. $\begin{array}{r} 363 \\ \times\ 8 \\ \hline \end{array}$	**14.** $\begin{array}{r} 249 \\ \times\ 10 \\ \hline \end{array}$	**15.** $\begin{array}{r} 803 \\ \times\ 3 \\ \hline \end{array}$	**16.** $\begin{array}{r} 349 \\ \times\ 6 \\ \hline \end{array}$

Moonlight Multiplication

Multiply to solve each problem.

1. 25
× 15

2. 341
× 35

3. 269
× 21

4. 456
× 18

5. 179
× 32

6. 1,023
× 24

7. 839
× 25

8. 214
× 58

9. 475
× 46

10. 245
× 103

11. 257
× 61

12. 2,435
× 14

Remainder Riddle

Use long division to solve each problem. Each answer will have a remainder. Find the remainder below and write the letter to solve the riddle. The first one is done for you.

1.

$$\begin{array}{r} 31R1 \\ 4\overline{)125} \\ -12 \\ \hline 5 \\ -4 \\ \hline 1 \end{array}$$

D

2. $5\overline{)264}$

D

3. $9\overline{)3,490}$

I

4. $9\overline{)341}$

O

5. $8\overline{)389}$

E

6. $6\overline{)2,588}$

A

7. $7\overline{)1,501}$

N

8. $7\overline{)1,329}$

L

9. $11\overline{)141}$

N

What kind of lion never bites or growls?

A <u> D </u> ___ ___ ___ ___ ___ ___ ___
   R1   R2   R3   R4   R5   R6   R7   R8   R9

Division Drill

Use long division to solve each problem.

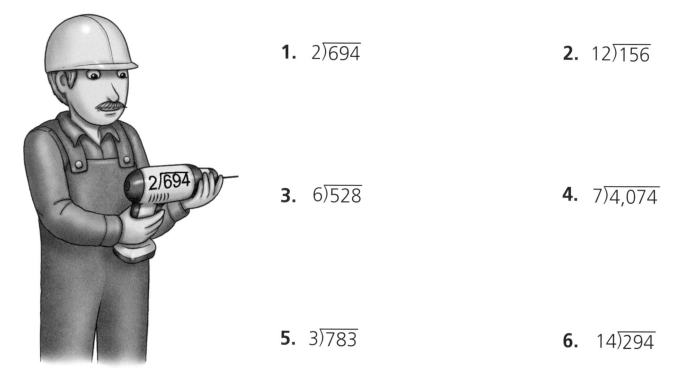

1. $2\overline{)694}$

2. $12\overline{)156}$

3. $6\overline{)528}$

4. $7\overline{)4,074}$

5. $3\overline{)783}$

6. $14\overline{)294}$

Use the long-division problems above to solve the multiplication problems below.

7. 261
   $\times\ \ \ 3$

8. 88
   $\times\ \ 6$

9. 582
   $\times\ \ \ 7$

10.   21
   $\times\ 14$

11. 347
   $\times\ \ 2$

12.   13
   $\times\ 12$

Zack's Snacks

Solve each problem.

1. It's Zack's turn to bring snacks for soccer practice, and he wants to bring pretzels. There are 26 kids on the soccer team. He wants to give each team member 20 pretzels. The pretzels are sold in bags of 200. How many bags of pretzels does he need to buy, and how many pretzels will be left over?

_____

2. A small box of granola bars comes with 6 bars. The jumbo-size box comes with 10 bars. Zack bought both small and jumbo-size boxes to get exactly 42 granola bars. How many small boxes and how many jumbo-size boxes did he buy?

_____

3. Zack used peanuts, raisins, and chocolate chips to make some trail mix. The recipe says that the number of raisins should be triple the number of chocolate chips. The recipe also says there should be twice as many peanuts as there are raisins. Zack put 282 raisins in the trail mix. How many chocolate chips and peanuts should there be?

_____

4. Zack poured juice into special trays to make his own ice pops. He can make 6 ice pops in each tray. He wants to make 28 ice pops for his party. How many trays does he need?

_____

True or False?

Read each sentence and circle *true* or *false*.

1. 3, 9, and 1 are factors of 9.   true   false

2. 91 is a prime number.   true   false

3. 125 is a multiple of 3.   true   false

4. 5, 2, 10, and 1 are factors of 10.   true   false

5. 36 is a multiple of both 3 and 8.   true   false

6. 23 is a prime number.   true   false

7. The number 18 has 6 factors.   true   false

8. 11 and 13 are both prime numbers.   true   false

9. All multiples of 2 are even numbers.   true   false

10. 21 only has two factors: 1 and 21.   true   false

11. 84, 98, and 106 are all multiples of 7.   true   false

12. All multiples of 3 are odd numbers.   true   false

Factor Trees

Fill in the missing numbers for each factor tree.

You can use a factor tree to break down a number into factors.

```
        12                12
       /  \              /  \
      6    ②          ③    4
     / \                    / \
    ③   ②                ②   ②
```

12 = 3 × 2 × 2   12 = 3 × 2 × 2

No matter how you break it down, you get the same numbers at the bottom. Multiply all the numbers at the bottom together to equal the number at the top of the tree.

1.

```
        36
       /  \
      9    □
     / \   / \
    3  □  2  2
```

2.

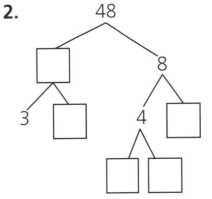

3.

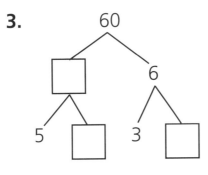

4.

```
        78
       /  \
      2    □
           / \
          3   □
```

Multiplication Market

Multiply to solve each problem. Don't forget to regroup and to place the decimal point in the correct spot.

1. $3.29
× 8

2. 16.42
× 5

3. $0.99
× 4

4. $4.79
× 6

5. 21.35
× 15

6. $2.85
× 11

7. $22.50
× 9

8. 132.65
× 3

9. $0.79
× 35

10. $4.70
× 6.5

11. 235.6
× 24

12. $5.50
× 1.5

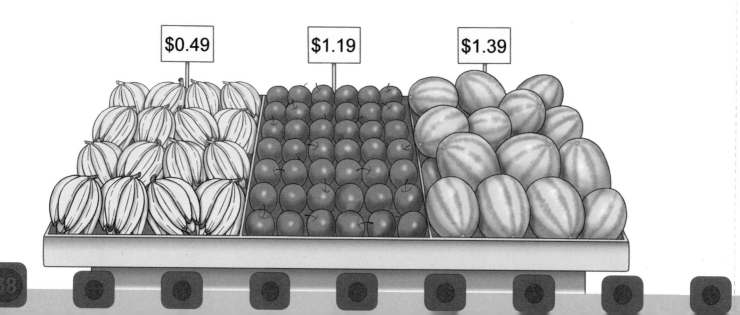

$0.49 $1.19 $1.39

Whose Shoes?

Read the sentences below to figure out who bought each pair of shoes.
Write the person's name by the correct pair of shoes.

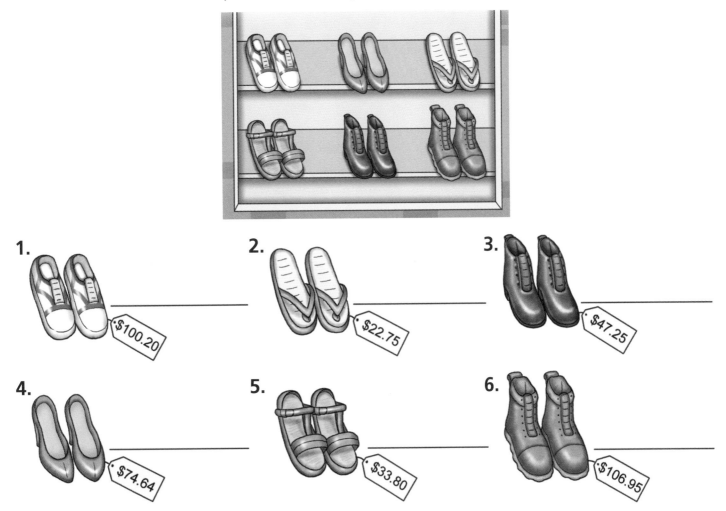

1. _____ $100.20

2. _____ $22.75

3. _____ $47.25

4. _____ $74.64

5. _____ $33.80

6. _____ $106.95

Lisa paid for her shoes with 6 five-dollar bills, 15 quarters, and 1 nickel.

Josh made $5.25 for each lawn he mowed. He mowed 9 lawns to earn exactly enough money for these shoes.

Ethan's three brothers each paid $35.65 to buy him these shoes for his birthday.

Sara paid for her shoes with 4 five-dollar bills, 2 one-dollar bills, and 3 quarters.

Jared saved $8.35 a week for 12 weeks to pay for his shoes.

Dawn saved $12.44 a week for 6 weeks to buy her shoes.

Decimal Disco

Multiply or divide to solve the problems.

1. 6.84
× 21

2. 3)14.4

3. 2.5
× 3.5

4. 6)144.78

5. 415.67
× 13

6. 12.8
× 1.4

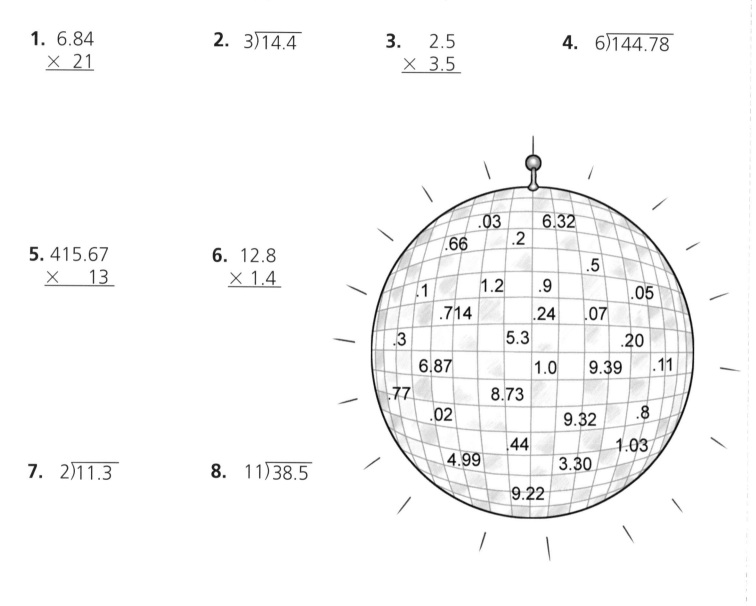

7. 2)11.3

8. 11)38.5

9. 567.02
× 10

10. 309.23
× 12

11. 8)132

12. 1.08
× 2.25

The Track Meet

Solve each problem.

1. The relay team finished the 4 x 100 meter relay in 70 seconds. If all 4 runners ran at the exact same pace, how long did it take each runner to complete his or her leg of the relay?

_____

2. Track Meet T-shirts were for sale for $15.75 each. Five runners decided to buy one for their coach. They split the cost equally. How much did each runner pay?

_____

3. Katie can run the 100-meter race in 16.28 seconds. How long would it take her to run a 400-meter race if she runs at the exact same pace?

_____

4. Each runner is charged a registration fee of $22.25 to enter the track meet. There are 24 kids on the school track team. To cover the cost of the registration fee, the team has decided to have a car wash. They are going to charge $6.00 per car. How many cars will they need to wash to earn enough to cover the registration cost for all the runners?

_____

Looking Shady

Find the fraction or decimal that does not match the picture and cross it out.

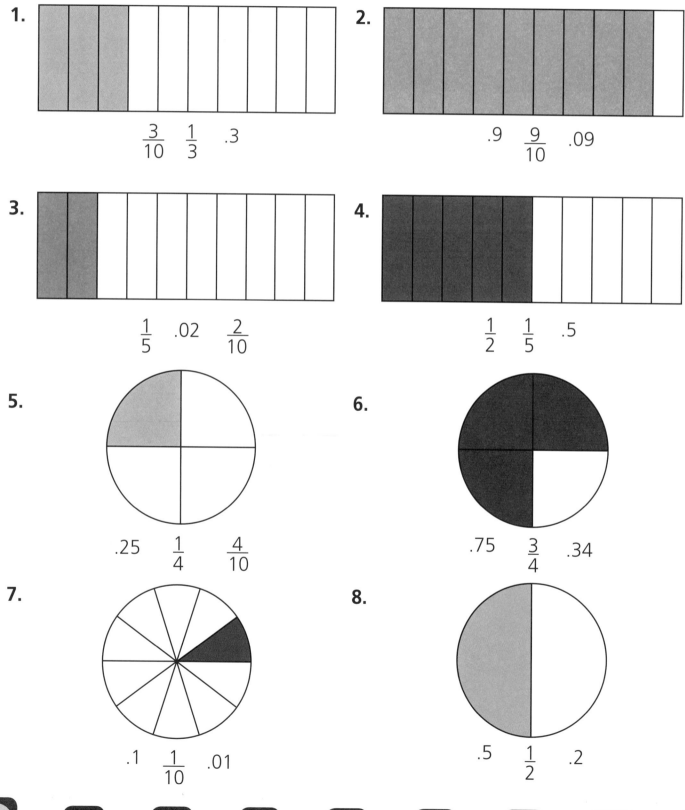

1.

$\frac{3}{10}$ $\frac{1}{3}$ .3

2.

.9 $\frac{9}{10}$ .09

3.

$\frac{1}{5}$ .02 $\frac{2}{10}$

4.

$\frac{1}{2}$ $\frac{1}{5}$ .5

5.

.25 $\frac{1}{4}$ $\frac{4}{10}$

6.

.75 $\frac{3}{4}$ .34

7.

.1 $\frac{1}{10}$ .01

8.

.5 $\frac{1}{2}$ .2

Fraction Find

Find the row with three equivalent fractions and circle it.
The row can go across, down, or diagonally.

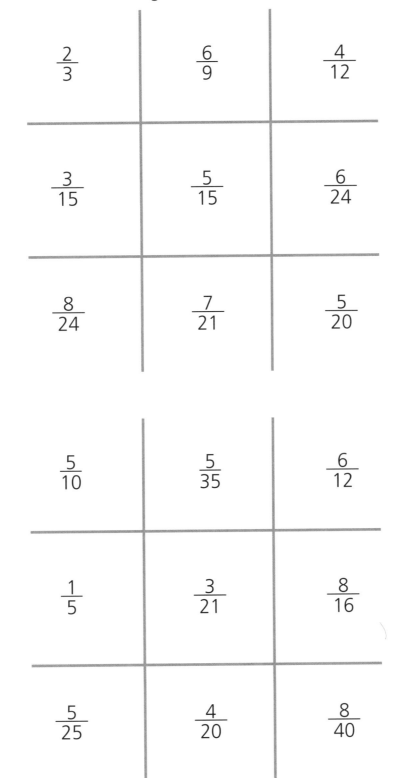

$\frac{2}{3}$	$\frac{6}{9}$	$\frac{4}{12}$
$\frac{3}{15}$	$\frac{5}{15}$	$\frac{6}{24}$
$\frac{8}{24}$	$\frac{7}{21}$	$\frac{5}{20}$

$\frac{5}{10}$	$\frac{5}{35}$	$\frac{6}{12}$
$\frac{1}{5}$	$\frac{3}{21}$	$\frac{8}{16}$
$\frac{5}{25}$	$\frac{4}{20}$	$\frac{8}{40}$

In the Same Boat

Write a decimal to equal each fraction. The first one is done for you.

1. $\frac{2}{10}$ = .2

2. $\frac{4}{100}$ = _____

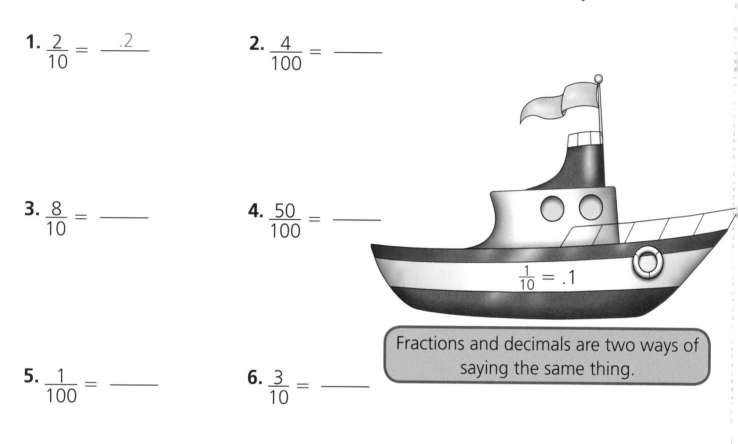

$\frac{1}{10}$ = .1

3. $\frac{8}{10}$ = _____

4. $\frac{50}{100}$ = _____

Fractions and decimals are two ways of saying the same thing.

5. $\frac{1}{100}$ = _____

6. $\frac{3}{10}$ = _____

Write a fraction to equal each decimal. The first one is done for you.

7. .06 = $\frac{6}{100}$ or $\frac{3}{50}$

8. .4 = _____ or _____

9. .09 = _____

10. .7 = _____

11. .03 = _____

12. .80 = _____ or _____

Laugh Lines

Write the numbers from the sun on the number line in order from least to greatest. Then use the code to solve the joke below.

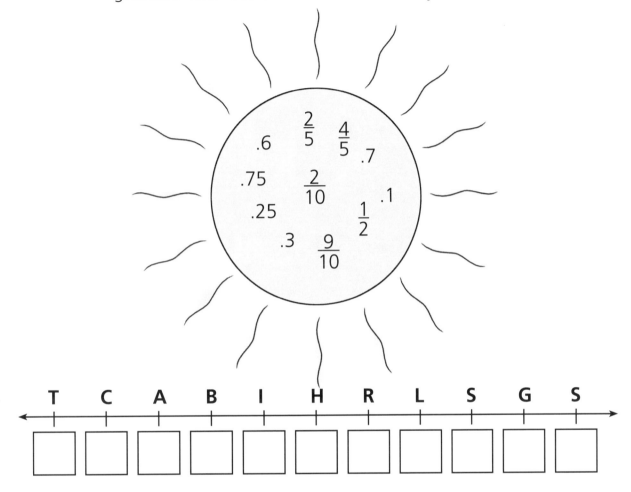

.6 $\frac{2}{5}$ $\frac{4}{5}$ .7   .75 $\frac{2}{10}$ .1   .25 $\frac{1}{2}$ .3 $\frac{9}{10}$

T   C   A   B   I   H   R   L   S   G   S

Why did the teacher wear sunglasses?

Because she had such a

___ ___ ___ ___ ___ ___   ___ ___ ___ ___ ___
.3   .6 $\frac{2}{5}$ $\frac{4}{5}$ $\frac{1}{2}$ .1 $\frac{2}{10}$ .7   .25 $\frac{9}{10}$ .75

45

The Change Challenge

Change each fraction into a decimal. The first one is done for you.

1. $\dfrac{1}{5}$ = __.2__

2. $\dfrac{19}{100}$ = _____

3. $\dfrac{1}{4}$ = _____

4. $\dfrac{37}{100}$ = _____

5. $\dfrac{10}{25}$ = _____

6. $\dfrac{3}{5}$ = _____

Change each decimal into a fraction. Write the fraction in lowest terms.

7. .75 = _____

8. .05 = _____

9. .21 = _____

10. .4 = _____

11. .66 = _____

12. .09 = _____

Recipe Riddles

Solve each problem.

1. Laura wants to make 3 hamburger patties. Each patty should have $\frac{1}{4}$ pound of beef. The grocery store had three packages of beef for sale. One was labeled .34 pounds, one was labeled .75 pounds, and one was labeled .25 pounds. Which one should she buy?

_____

2. Kelly picked 100 oranges to squeeze for orange juice. Of the 100 oranges, 5 weren't ripe yet and could not be used. What fraction of the oranges were not ripe? Write the amount as a decimal and as a fraction.

_____

3. Andrew baked a loaf of bread and cut it into 10 slices. He gave 3 slices to Chris. What fraction of the bread did he give away? Write the amount as a decimal.

_____

4. Lenny has three fish recipes. The recipe for fish stew calls for $\frac{1}{2}$ pound fish. The recipe for fish cakes calls for $\frac{3}{4}$ pounds of fish. And the recipe for fish tacos calls for $\frac{1}{4}$ pound of fish. Lenny has a package of fish that weighs .41 pounds. Which recipe does he have enough fish to make?

_____

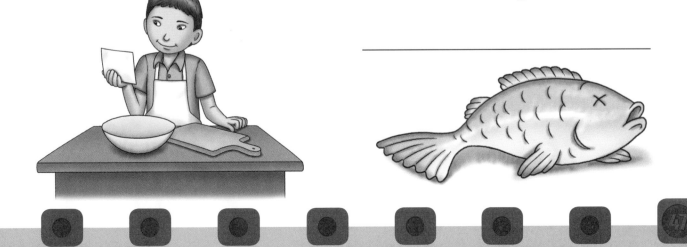

All Mixed Up

Write each improper fraction as a mixed fraction.

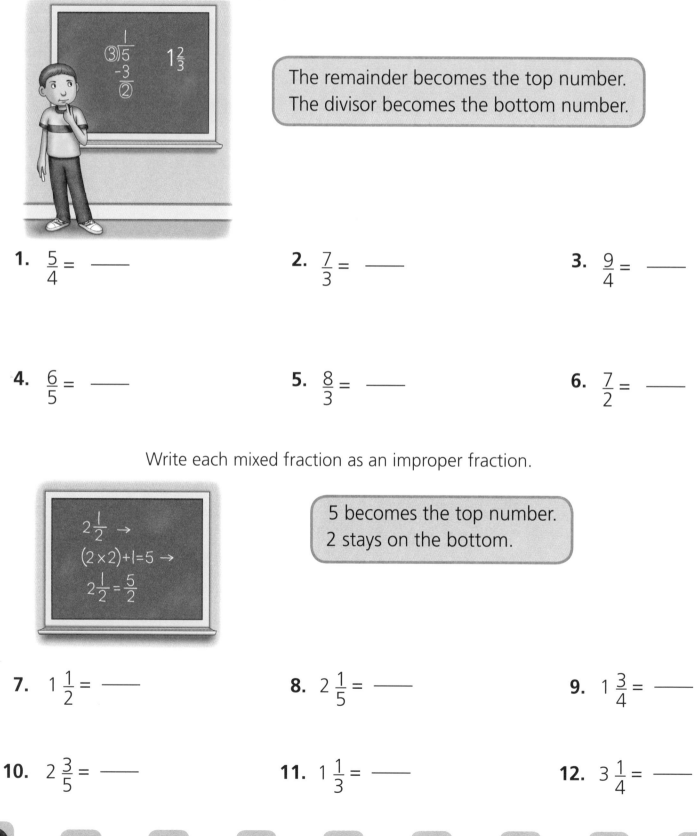

1. $\dfrac{5}{4} =$ _____

2. $\dfrac{7}{3} =$ _____

3. $\dfrac{9}{4} =$ _____

4. $\dfrac{6}{5} =$ _____

5. $\dfrac{8}{3} =$ _____

6. $\dfrac{7}{2} =$ _____

Write each mixed fraction as an improper fraction.

> 5 becomes the top number.
> 2 stays on the bottom.

7. $1\dfrac{1}{2} =$ _____

8. $2\dfrac{1}{5} =$ _____

9. $1\dfrac{3}{4} =$ _____

10. $2\dfrac{3}{5} =$ _____

11. $1\dfrac{1}{3} =$ _____

12. $3\dfrac{1}{4} =$ _____

Cross-Number Puzzle

Change each fraction or mixed fraction into a decimal and write it in the cross-number puzzle. Use one box for a decimal point.

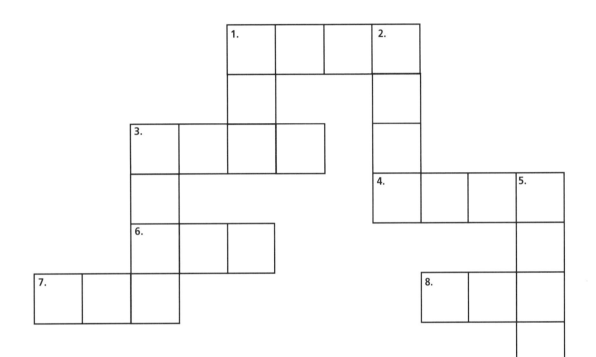

Across

1. $1\frac{13}{100}$

3. $1\frac{3}{4}$

4. $5\frac{3}{4}$

6. $2\frac{1}{10}$

7. $2\frac{1}{2}$

8. $1\frac{1}{5}$

Down

1. $1\frac{7}{10}$

2. $3\frac{1}{4}$

3. $1\frac{1}{4}$

5. $5\frac{21}{100}$

Nothing in Common

Find the lowest number that both denominators can divide into.

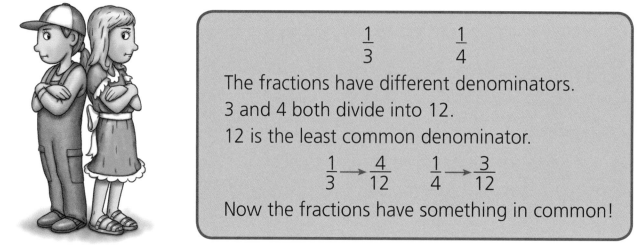

$$\frac{1}{3} \qquad \frac{1}{4}$$

The fractions have different denominators.
3 and 4 both divide into 12.
12 is the least common denominator.

$$\frac{1}{3} \longrightarrow \frac{4}{12} \qquad \frac{1}{4} \longrightarrow \frac{3}{12}$$

Now the fractions have something in common!

Find the least common denominator for each pair of fractions. Then rewrite the two fractions so they have the same denominator. The first one is done for you.

1. $\frac{2}{5}$ and $\frac{1}{10}$

Least Common Denominator: _10_

$\frac{4}{10}$ $\frac{1}{10}$

2. $\frac{1}{3}$ and $\frac{1}{2}$

Least Common Denominator: ____

____   ____

3. $\frac{3}{4}$ and $\frac{1}{8}$

Least Common Denominator: ____

____   ____

4. $\frac{1}{5}$ and $\frac{1}{4}$

Least Common Denominator: ____

____   ____

5. $\frac{5}{8}$ and $\frac{5}{6}$

Least Common Denominator: ____

____   ____

6. $\frac{2}{3}$ and $\frac{3}{5}$

Least Common Denominator: ____

____   ____

7. $\frac{1}{6}$ and $\frac{3}{12}$

Least Common Denominator: ____

____   ____

8. $\frac{2}{9}$ and $\frac{1}{3}$

Least Common Denominator: ____

____   ____

Fraction Flowers

Half of the flowers below have fractions expressed in lowest terms. The other half are not in lowest terms. Circle all the lowest terms fractions and list them below.

Friendly Fractions

Convert the fractions so the denominators are the same. Then add or subtract.
The first one is done for you.

1. $\dfrac{2}{3} - \dfrac{1}{9} = \dfrac{6}{9} - \dfrac{1}{9} = \dfrac{5}{9}$

2. $\dfrac{1}{8} + \dfrac{1}{4} = \underline{} + \underline{} = \underline{}$

3. $\dfrac{1}{15} + \dfrac{1}{5} = \underline{} + \underline{} = \underline{}$

4. $\dfrac{7}{10} - \dfrac{1}{5} = \underline{} - \underline{} = \underline{}$ or $\underline{}$

5. $\dfrac{3}{4} + \dfrac{2}{3} = \underline{} + \underline{} = \underline{}$ or $\underline{}$

6. $\dfrac{1}{4} - \dfrac{1}{6} = \underline{} - \underline{} = \underline{}$

7. $\dfrac{4}{5} - \dfrac{1}{2} = \underline{} - \underline{} = \underline{}$

8. $\dfrac{11}{12} - \dfrac{5}{6} = \underline{} - \underline{} = \underline{}$

9. $\dfrac{1}{8} + \dfrac{1}{6} = \underline{} + \underline{} = \underline{}$

10. $\dfrac{1}{10} + \dfrac{3}{8} = \underline{} + \underline{} = \underline{}$

11. $\dfrac{5}{6} - \dfrac{5}{9} = \underline{} - \underline{} = \underline{}$

12. $\dfrac{1}{4} + \dfrac{3}{10} = \underline{} + \underline{} = \underline{}$

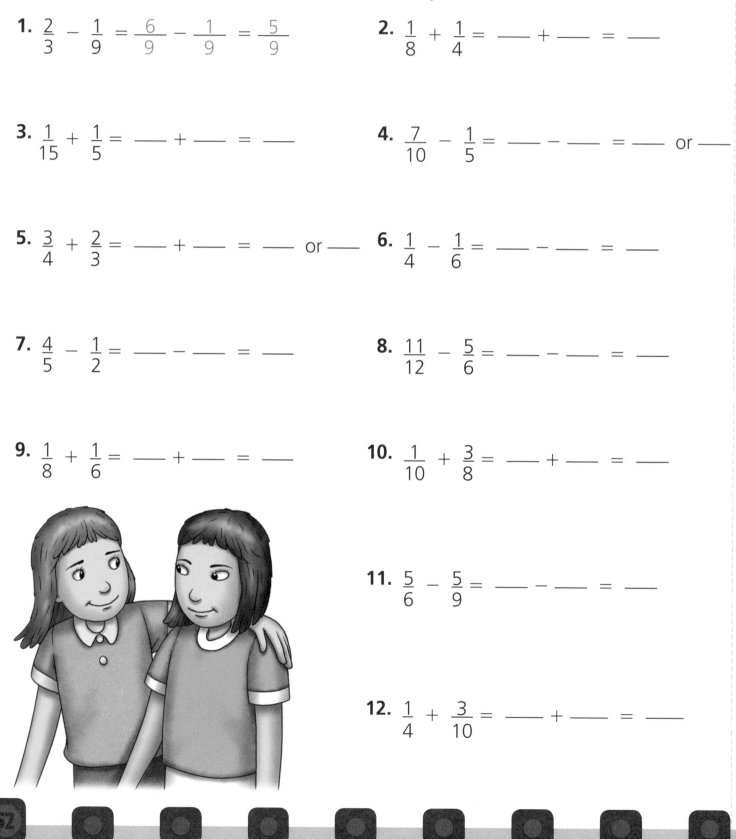

What's Cooking?

Solve each problem.

1. Mary has three kinds of nuts to mix into her batter. She has $\frac{1}{2}$ cup of almonds, $\frac{3}{8}$ cup of walnuts, and $\frac{5}{4}$ cups of pecans. List the nuts in order from the least to the greatest amount.

_____

_____

_____

2. There was $\frac{3}{4}$ cup sugar left in the pantry. Erin used $\frac{1}{8}$ cup of the sugar to bake muffins. Henry sprinkled $\frac{1}{8}$ cup on his strawberries. Greg needs $\frac{1}{2}$ cup sugar to bake brownies. Is there enough left for Greg to bake the brownies?

_____

3. Jack's recipe calls for 1.25 cups of berries. Jack can find only one measuring cup—the $\frac{1}{4}$ cup. How many $\frac{1}{4}$ cups of berries would be the same as 1.25?

_____

4. Nina found four packages of meat in the freezer. She found 1.4 pounds of chicken, $\frac{1}{2}$ pound of beef, $1\frac{1}{4}$ pounds of pork, and .8 pounds of turkey. List the meats in order from the greatest amount to the least.

_____

_____

_____

_____

Piano Practice

Margot's pictograph shows how many minutes she practiced piano for each day.
Use the graph to answer the questions.

Monday	♪ ♪
Tuesday	♪ ♪ ♪
Wednesday	♪
Thursday	♪ ♪ ♪ ♪
Friday	♪ ♪ ♪ ♪ ♪

♪ = 15 minutes

1. How many more minutes did she practice on Friday than on Tuesday?

_____

2. How many hours did Margot practice on Thursday? _____

3. On how many days was Margot's practice time shorter than one hour?

_____

4. On Saturday, Margot practiced for an hour and a half. How many notes should
go on the pictograph for Saturday? _____

5. How many minutes total did Margot practice Monday through Friday?

_____

6. Next week, Margot wants to practice for 150 minutes. She wants to practice
for the same number of minutes each day, Monday through Friday. How many
notes will be on the pictograph for each day? _____

Desert Drops

The bar graph shows how many inches of rain fell in the desert last year.
Use the graph to answer the questions below.

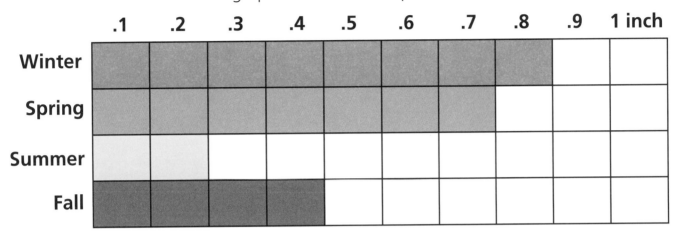

1. Which season received $\frac{1}{5}$ inch of rain? _____

2. How much rain fell during winter and spring combined?

_____

3. How much more rain fell in the spring than in summer?

_____

4. Which two seasons combined total exactly one inch of rain?

_____

5. Write the increase in rainfall from fall to winter as a fraction and as a decimal.

_____

6. Write the total amount of rainfall for the year as a fraction and as a decimal.

_____

It Figures!

Find the area for each figure.

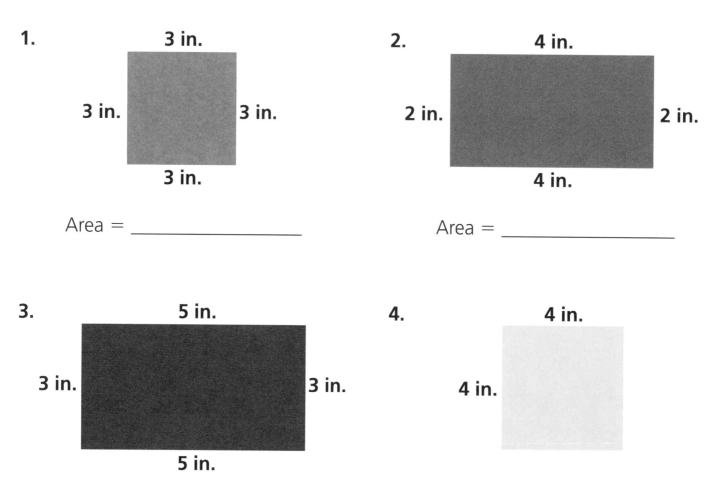

1.

3 in.

3 in.   3 in.

3 in.

Area = _____

2.

4 in.

2 in.   2 in.

4 in.

Area = _____

3.

5 in.

3 in.   3 in.

5 in.

Area = _____

4.

4 in.

4 in.

Area = _____

5. The area of a square is 36 inches squared. What is the length of one side?

_____

6. A rectangle is 10 feet long and 4 feet wide. What is the area?

Area = _____

Perimeter Puzzle

Find the perimeter of each shape. Find the row with three shapes that have equal perimeters. The row can go across, down, or diagonally.

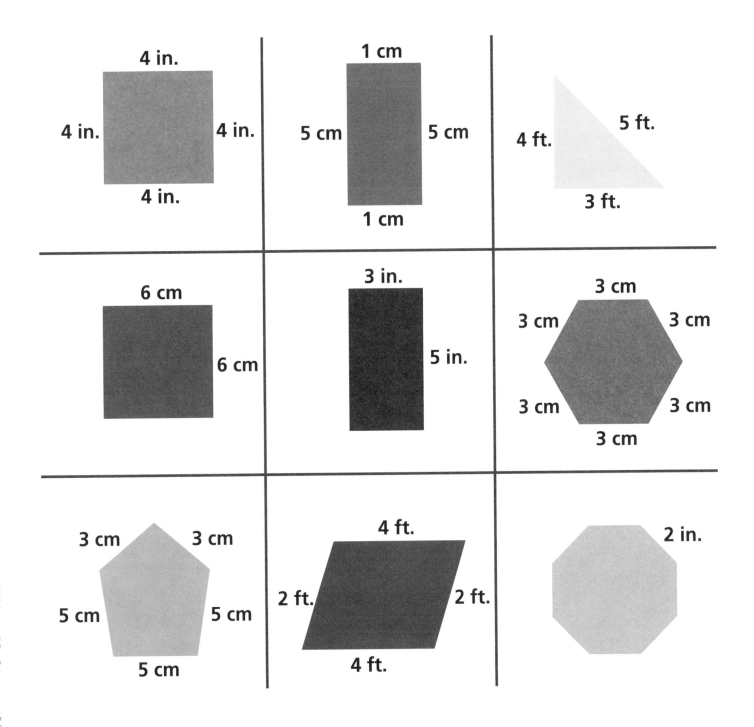

Circle of Friends

Find the diameter for each circle.

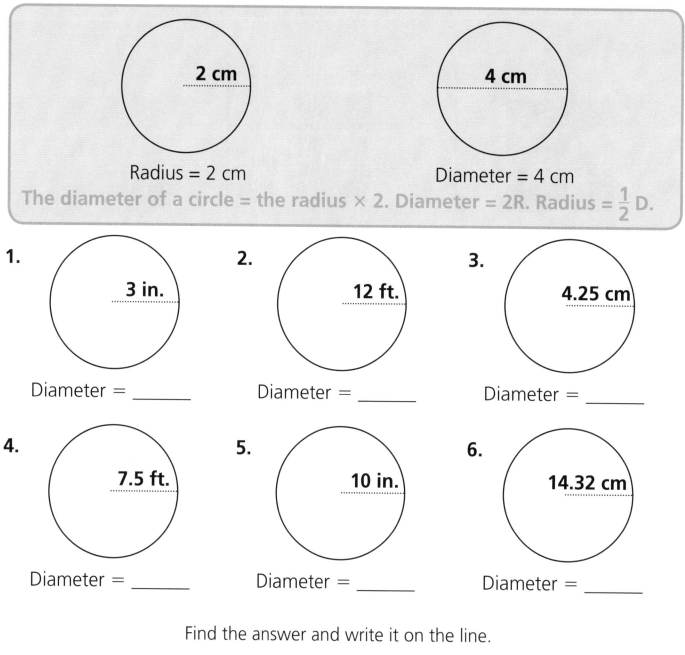

Radius = 2 cm

Diameter = 4 cm

The diameter of a circle = the radius × 2. Diameter = 2R. Radius = $\frac{1}{2}$ D.

1.

3 in.

Diameter = _____

2.

12 ft.

Diameter = _____

3.

4.25 cm

Diameter = _____

4.

7.5 ft.

Diameter = _____

5.

10 in.

Diameter = _____

6.

14.32 cm

Diameter = _____

Find the answer and write it on the line.

7. The diameter of a circle is 20 inches. What is the radius?_____

8. A circle has a radius of 3.22 centimeters. What is the diameter?_____

9. The radius of a circle measures 506.21 feet. What is the diameter?_____

Area Code

Find the area of each shape. You will need to break down each figure into smaller shapes and find the area of each shape. The first problem is done for you.

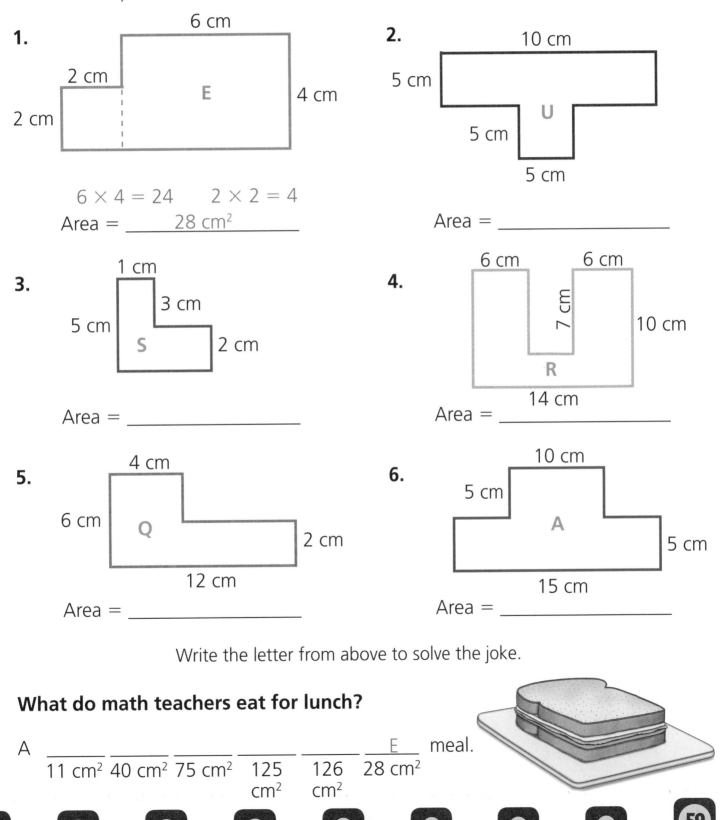

1.

6 cm

2 cm

E

4 cm

2 cm

2 cm

$6 \times 4 = 24$ $2 \times 2 = 4$

Area = ___28 cm²___

2.

10 cm

5 cm

U

5 cm

5 cm

Area = _____

3.

1 cm

3 cm

5 cm

S

2 cm

Area = _____

4.

6 cm   6 cm

7 cm

10 cm

R

14 cm

Area = _____

5.

4 cm

6 cm

Q

2 cm

12 cm

Area = _____

6.

10 cm

5 cm

A

5 cm

15 cm

Area = _____

Write the letter from above to solve the joke.

What do math teachers eat for lunch?

A ____ ____ ____ ____ ____ __E__ meal.

 11 cm² 40 cm² 75 cm² 125 cm² 126 cm² 28 cm²

Bent Out of Shape

Study the figures. Some are 3D shapes and some are nets for 3D shapes. Find the word that matches each figure and write it on the line.

rectangular prism	cube	cylinder
pyramid	sphere	cone

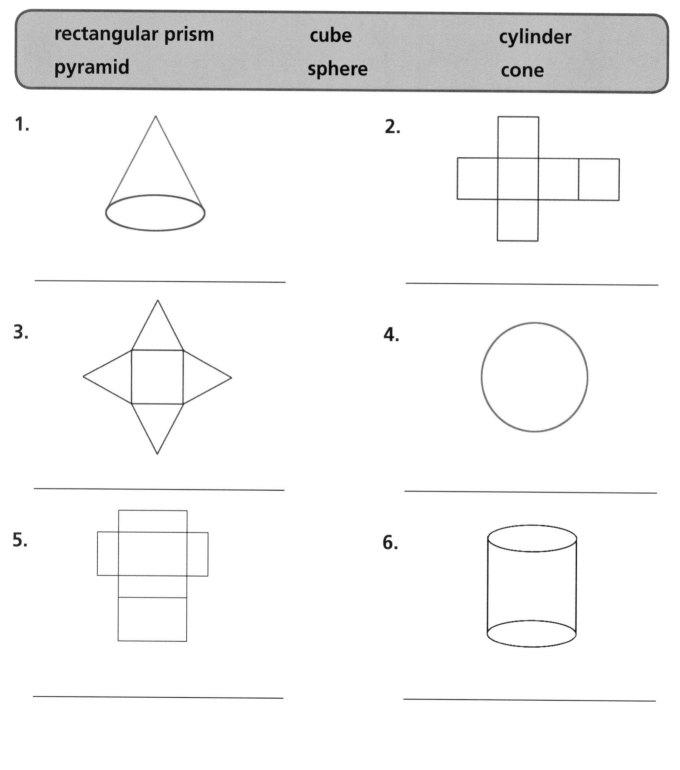

1. _____

2. _____

3. _____

4. _____

5. _____

6. _____

Sporting Solutions

Solve each problem.

1. Kim can go jogging at Overland Field or Westwood Field. Both rectangular fields have an area of 2,000 square feet. Overland Field measures 40 feet wide. Westwood Field measures 25 feet wide. Find the length of each field, then calculate the perimeter of both fields. Which field should she jog around to get the longer run?

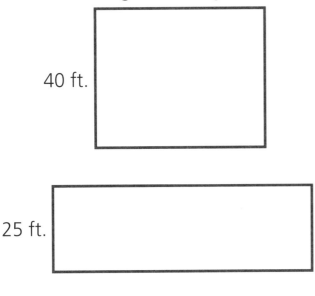

40 ft.

25 ft.

_____

3. Steve wants to run a total of 1,000 yards. He is on a field that is 75 feet long and 50 feet wide. How many times does he need to run around the perimeter of the field?

_____

2. The coach asked the students to stand in a circle. If he blew the whistle once, a student had to run in a straight line 20 feet to the center of the circle. If he blew the whistle twice, a student had to run through the center in a straight line to the other edge of the circle. How far did the student run when the coach blew the whistle twice?

_____

4. The basketball team can practice on the indoor court or the outdoor court. The two courts have the same perimeter—200 feet. The indoor court is 60 feet wide and the outdoor court is 50 feet wide. Find the length of each court, then calculate the area. The team wants to use the court with the greatest area. Which court should they use?

_____

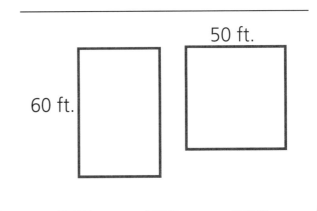

50 ft.

60 ft.

Angle Wrangle

Label each angle as *right*, *acute*, or *obtuse*.

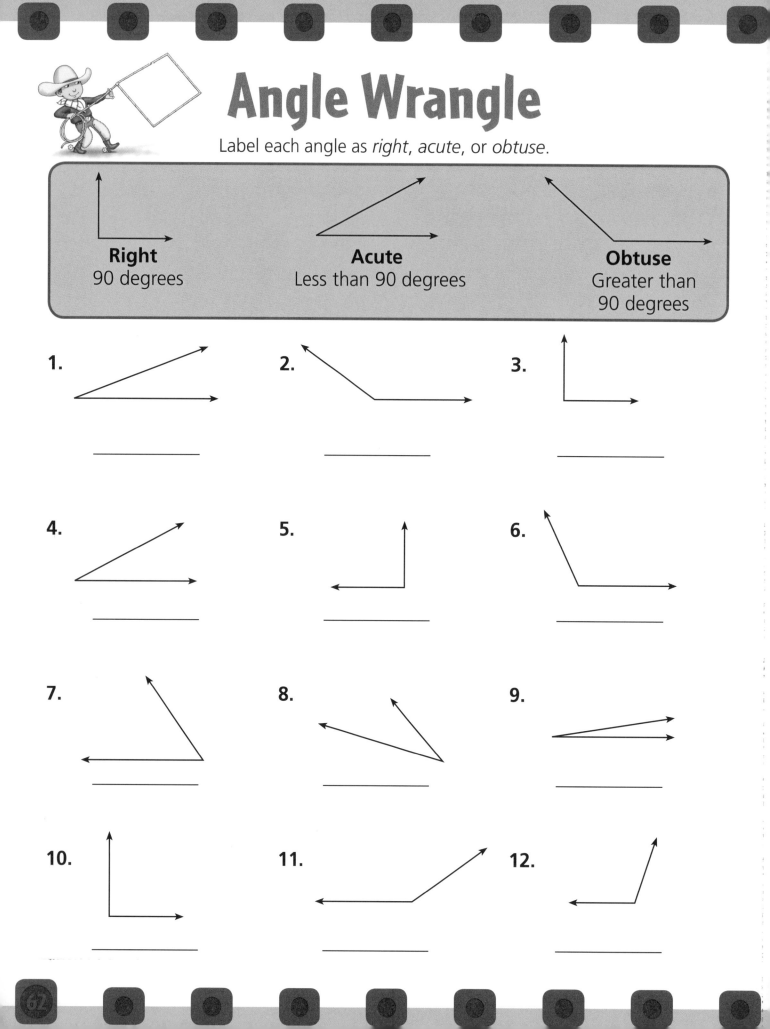

Right
90 degrees

Acute
Less than 90 degrees

Obtuse
Greater than
90 degrees

1.

_____

2.

_____

3.

_____

4.

_____

5.

_____

6.

_____

7.

_____

8.

_____

9.

_____

10.

_____

11.

_____

12.

_____

Crossword Puzzle

Use the clues below to fill in the correct words for the crossword puzzle.

Across
1. Squares, rectangles, and rhombuses are all examples of this shape.
4. A triangle with two sides of equal length.
6. A three-dimensional shape with six square faces.
7. A shape like this: ⏢
8. A triangle with all three sides of different lengths.

Down
2. A shape like this: ▱
3. A triangle with all three sides of equal length.
5. A shape with four equal sides and four right angles.

Look Alikes

Look at each pair of shapes. If they are the exact same size and shape, circle *congruent*. If not, circle *non-congruent*.

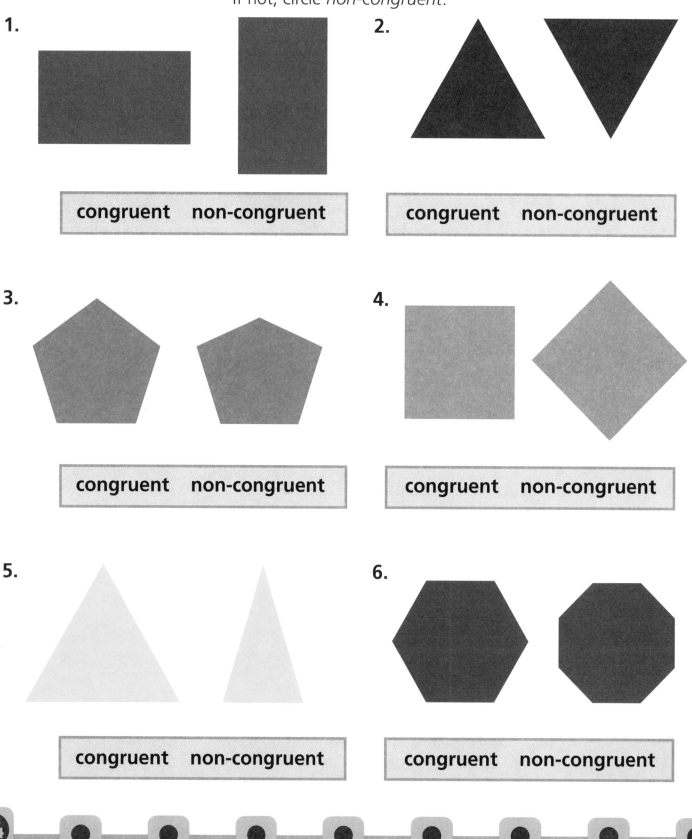

1.

congruent   non-congruent

2.

congruent   non-congruent

3.

congruent   non-congruent

4.

congruent   non-congruent

5.

congruent   non-congruent

6.

congruent   non-congruent

A Silver Lining

Circle the clouds with parallel or perpendicular lines.

Symmetry Search

Find the figure that does NOT show a line of symmetry and circle it.

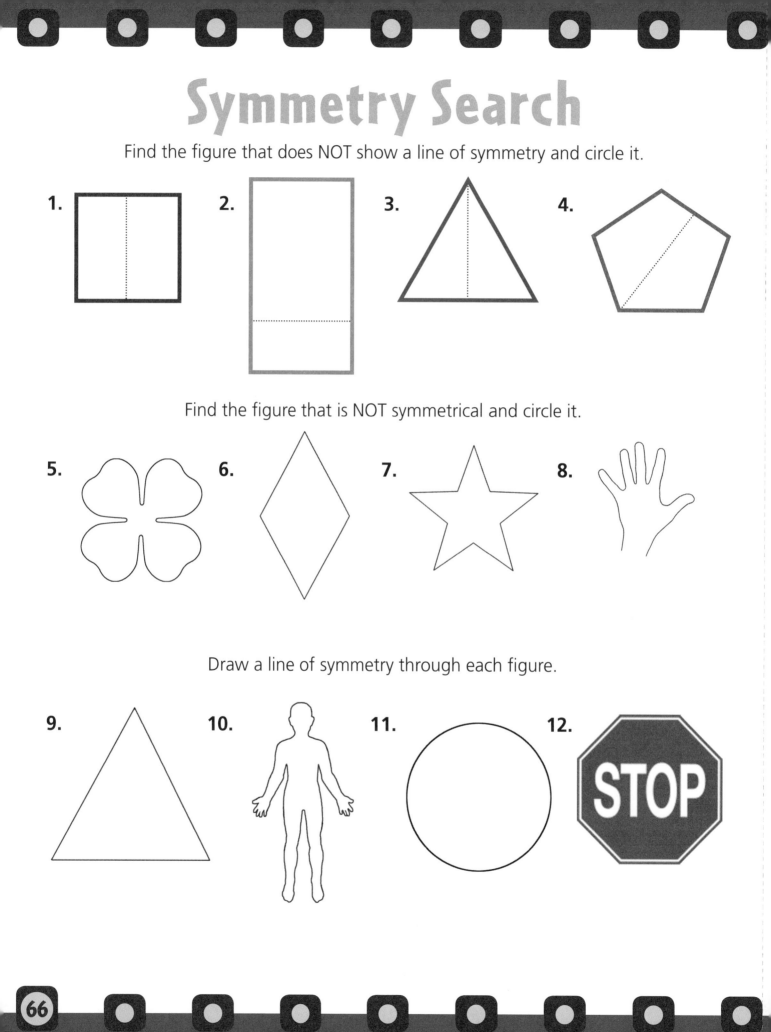

1.

2.

3.

4.

Find the figure that is NOT symmetrical and circle it.

5.

6.

7.

8.

Draw a line of symmetry through each figure.

9.

10.

11.

12.

STOP

Show the Shape

Solve the riddles and show what each shape or figure looks like.

1. I am a shape with three sides. All my sides are the same length. What am I? Give my name and draw a picture of me.

_____

draw shape here

2. We are two straight lines. We are always the same distance apart. We never cross over or intersect. What are we? Give our name and draw a picture of us.

_____

draw shape here

3. I am a triangle. Two of my sides are perpendicular lines. What am I? Give my name and draw a picture of me.

_____

4. I have four sides of equal lengths. I am not a square. I do not have any right angles. What am I? Give my name and draw a picture of me.

_____

draw shape here

draw shape here

What a Value!

Find the value for *n* in each problem.

1. $7 + n = 21$ $n =$ _____

2. $n - 18 = 49$ $n =$ _____

3. $12 \times n = 72$ $n =$ _____

4. $41 - n = 28$ $n =$ _____

5. $117 \div n = 9$ $n =$ _____

6. $7n = 56$ $n =$ _____

The value for *n* is shown in the box below.
Substitute the value for *n* and solve each problem.

$n = 8$

7. $48 \div n =$ _____

8. $4n =$ _____

9. $67 + n =$ _____

10. $n + n =$ _____

11. $n - 6 =$ _____

12. $n \times n =$ _____

$5 + n$

Game of the Same

Find three expressions in a row that are saying the same thing.
The row can go across, down, or diagonally.

7n	a number times 7	a number minus 7
7 − n	7 less than a number	n − 7
a number plus 7	n + 7	7 more than a number

n − 2	2 more than a number	2n
2 less than a number	2 + n	twice a number
n + n	2 − n	n × 2

First-Class Equations

Solve each equation.

Always do the problem inside the parentheses FIRST.
$$4 + (5 \overset{10}{\times} 2) = 4 + 10 = 14$$
$$(4 \overset{9}{+} 5) \times 2 = 9 \times 2 = 18$$

1. $4 + (24 \div 4) = $ _____

2. $(4 + 24) \div 4 = $ _____

3. $(18 - 7) + 5 = $ _____

4. $18 - (7 + 5) = $ _____

5. $30 - (5 \times 5) = $ _____

6. $(30 - 5) \times 5 = $ _____

7. $(30 - 15) \div 3 = $ _____

8. $30 - (15 \div 3) = $ _____

9. $6 \times (10 - 4) = $ _____

10. $(6 \times 10) - 4 = $ _____

11. $(5 \times 8) \div 4 = $ _____

12. $5 \times (8 \div 4) = $ _____

Value-Ball

To solve each problem, find the variable inside the net. Substitute the value for the letter and solve the equation. The first one is done for you.

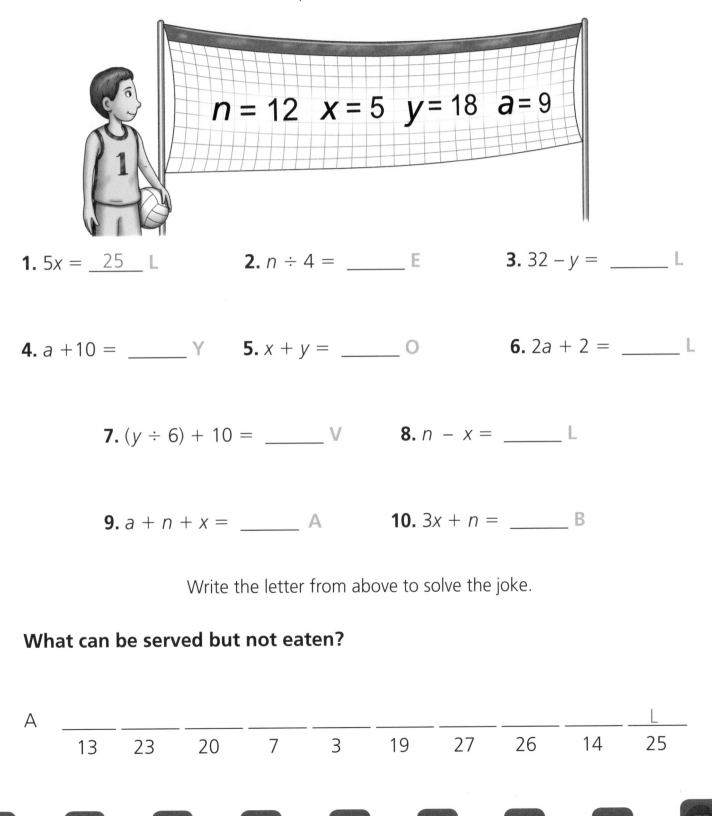

$n = 12 \quad x = 5 \quad y = 18 \quad a = 9$

1. $5x =$ __25__ **L**

2. $n \div 4 =$ _____ **E**

3. $32 - y =$ _____ **L**

4. $a + 10 =$ _____ **Y**

5. $x + y =$ _____ **O**

6. $2a + 2 =$ _____ **L**

7. $(y \div 6) + 10 =$ _____ **V**

8. $n - x =$ _____ **L**

9. $a + n + x =$ _____ **A**

10. $3x + n =$ _____ **B**

Write the letter from above to solve the joke.

What can be served but not eaten?

A ____ ____ ____ ____ ____ ____ ____ ____ ____ <u>L</u>
 13   23   20   7   3   19   27   26   14   25

Sign Sleuth

The operation signs are missing from the problems!
Substitute the value in the magnifying glass for *n*.
Fill in the sign that makes the math sentence true.

n = 6

1. $n \ \square \ 4 = 10$

2. $18 \ \square \ n = 3$

3. $n \ \square \ n = 36$

n = 10

4. $5 \ \square \ n = 50$

5. $n \ \square \ 7 = 3$

6. $n \ \square \ n = 20$

n = 15

7. $n \ \square \ 10 = 5$

8. $n \ \square \ 5 = 3$

9. $n \ \square \ n = 30$

n = 7

10. $n \ \square \ 5 = 35$

11. $14 \ \square \ n = 21$

12. $n \ \square \ n = 49$

Jessica's Juice Stand

Solve each problem.

1. Jessica's mother helped her start a juice stand. She loaned Jessica 4 dollars to buy the cups and $3.50 to buy the ingredients. Jessica sold 25 cups of juice for a dollar a cup. Which equation shows how much money she made after she paid back her mom for the supplies?

a) 25 + (4 − 3.50)

b) 25 − (4 + 3.50)

c) 25 − (4 − 3.50)

2. Jessica decided to sell juice in two sizes of cups. A small cup cost $0.75 and a large cup cost $1.50. A group came to the stand and ordered 6 small cups and 4 large cups of juice. Which equation would Jessica use to find how much to charge the group in all?

a) (6 × $0.75) + (4 × $1.50)

b) (4 + $1.50) × (6 + $0.75)

c) (6 + 0.75) × (4 + 1.50)

3. Jessica made orange juice and grapefruit juice. She sold 30 cups of orange juice for $1.25 each. She sold 18 cups of grapefruit juice for $1.75 per cup. Write a number sentence to find how much more money she made selling orange juice than grapefruit juice.

_____

4. Jessica used the juice of 18 oranges to make 1 quart of orange juice. She wants to make 6 quarts of orange juice. Write a number sentence to find how many oranges she needs to buy.

_____

Taking Sides

Read each number sentence carefully.
If both sides are equal, circle *true*. If not, circle *false*.

Equals added to equals are equal.	Equals multiplied by equals are equal.
$5 = 2 + 3$	$5 = 2 + 3$
$5 + 1 = (2 + 3) + 1$	$5 \times 5 = (2 + 3) \times 5$

1. $3 + 1 = (2 + 1) + 1$

    true   false

2. $4 \times 4 = (2 + 2) + 4$

    true   false

3. $7 + x = 7x$

    true   false

4. $5 + y = (2 + 3) + y$

    true   false

5. $10x = 10 \times (10 + x)$

    true   false

6. $12y = (3 \times 4)y$

    true   false

7. $8 \times 15 = 8 \times (3 \times 5)$

    true   false

8. $3 \times (5 + 4) = 3 \times 1$

    true   false

9. $6x + 7 = 6x + (3 + 4)$

    true   false

10. $(6 \times 3) + 10 = 9 + 10$

    true   false

11. $x + y = 2x + 2y$

    true   false

12. $11 \times 14 = 11 \times (7 + 7)$

    true   false

Figure out the Formula

Read the clues below and find the formula.
Fill in the correct words for the crossword puzzle.

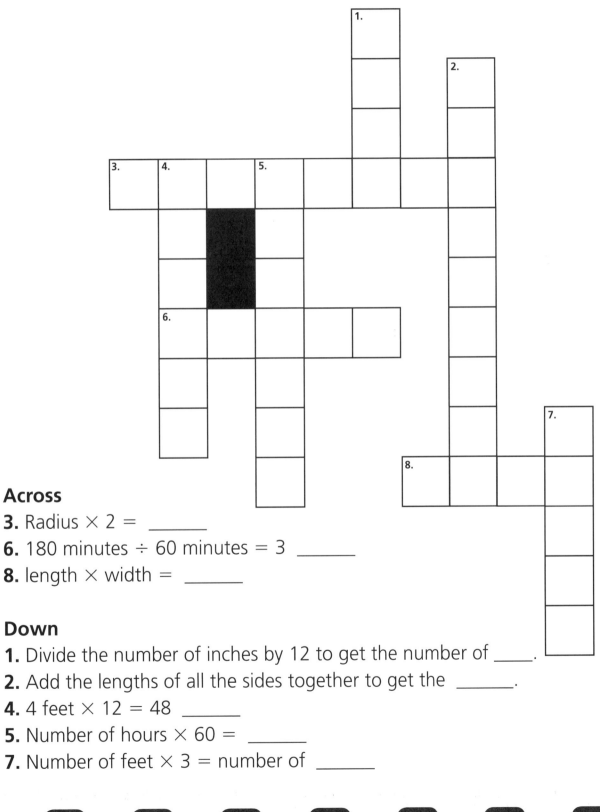

Across

3. Radius × 2 = _____

6. 180 minutes ÷ 60 minutes = 3 _____

8. length × width = _____

Down

1. Divide the number of inches by 12 to get the number of ____.

2. Add the lengths of all the sides together to get the _____.

4. 4 feet × 12 = 48 _____

5. Number of hours × 60 = _____

7. Number of feet × 3 = number of _____

Plug It In

Plug in the values for x and y to find the answer for each equation.

1. $5x + y =$ _____

2. $3x - y =$ _____

3. $10x + y =$ _____

4. $2x + 2y =$ _____

5. $4x - y =$ _____

6. $6x + y =$ _____

Now plug in the numeral 2 for the value of x.
Find the value of y for each problem.

$x = 2$

7. $3x + y = 10$ $y =$ _____

8. $7x + y = 20$ $y =$ _____

9. $4x - y = 5$ $y =$ _____

Now plug in the numeral 5 for the value of y.
Find the value of x for each problem.

$y = 5$

10. $2x + y = 19$ $x =$ _____

11. $6x - y = 7$ $x =$ _____

12. $3x + y = 14$ $x =$ _____

Where's the Pair?

Find the values for *x* and *y* that make each equation true. Draw a line to match each shoe with the correct sock. The first one is done for you.

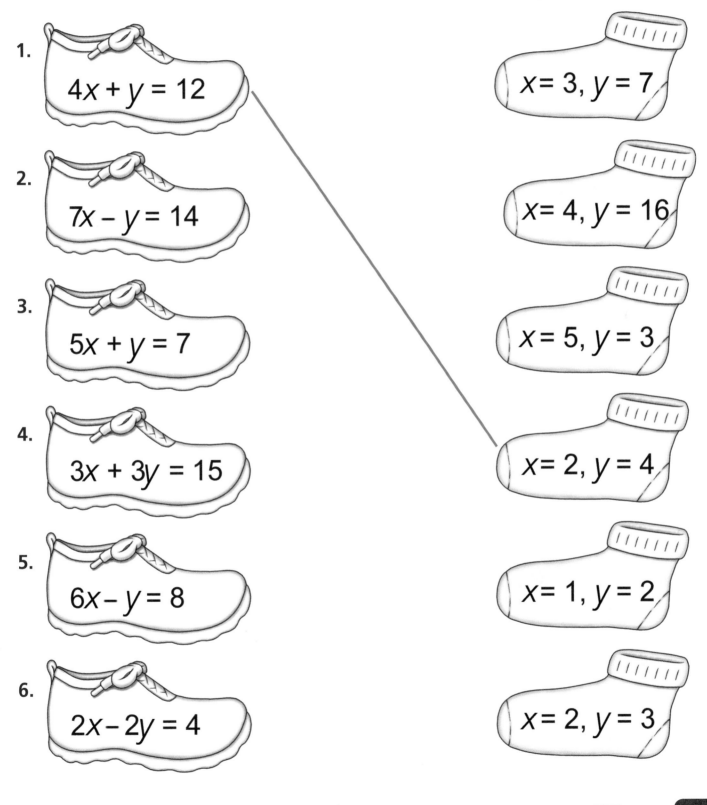

1. $4x + y = 12$

2. $7x - y = 14$

3. $5x + y = 7$

4. $3x + 3y = 15$

5. $6x - y = 8$

6. $2x - 2y = 4$

$x = 3, y = 7$

$x = 4, y = 16$

$x = 5, y = 3$

$x = 2, y = 4$

$x = 1, y = 2$

$x = 2, y = 3$

Who's on First?

Plug in the value for *x* and solve each equation.
Remember to do the problem inside the parentheses first.

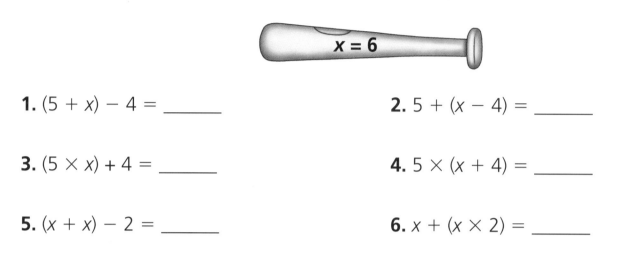

x = 6

1. $(5 + x) - 4 = $ _____

2. $5 + (x - 4) = $ _____

3. $(5 \times x) + 4 = $ _____

4. $5 \times (x + 4) = $ _____

5. $(x + x) - 2 = $ _____

6. $x + (x \times 2) = $ _____

Solve each equation for *x*. Find the correct answers inside the baseballs.

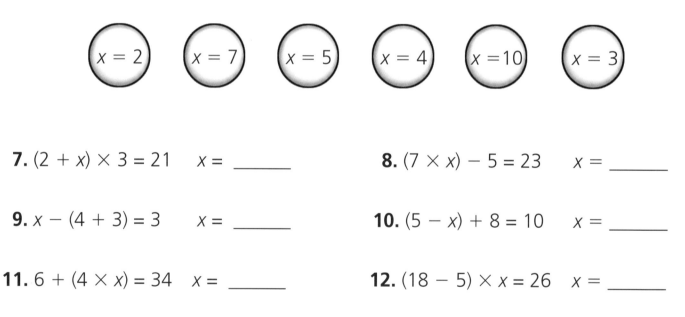

x = 2   *x* = 7   *x* = 5   *x* = 4   *x* = 10   *x* = 3

7. $(2 + x) \times 3 = 21$ *x* = _____

8. $(7 \times x) - 5 = 23$ *x* = _____

9. $x - (4 + 3) = 3$ *x* = _____

10. $(5 - x) + 8 = 10$ *x* = _____

11. $6 + (4 \times x) = 34$ *x* = _____

12. $(18 - 5) \times x = 26$ *x* = _____

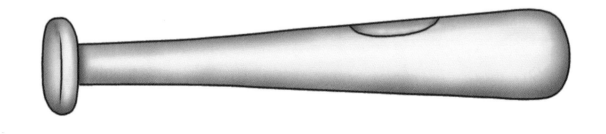

Name That Number!

Read the riddles and figure out which numbers are being described.
Name the numbers to solve each riddle.

1. We are two numbers.
Our product is 35. Our sum is 12.
What numbers are we?

_____

2. We are two odd numbers
Our sum is 16. Our difference is 2.
What numbers are we?

_____

3. I am an even number. Whether you
double me or just add 2 to me, you
get the same answer. What number
am I?

_____

4. We are three numbers. If you add us
together, you get 10. No matter
which order you multiply us, the
product is 30. Two of us added
together equal the third number.
What numbers are we?

_____

1   13   6   40   10   3

The Lunch Bunch

The chart shows the measurements of all the tables in the lunch area.
Use the chart to answer the questions below.

Table	Length	Width
A	10 feet	4 feet
B	8 feet	5 feet
C	6 feet	3 feet
D	9 feet	4 feet

1. Which two tables have the same area? _____

2. Which table has the longest perimeter? _____

3. Which table has the same number for its area and its perimeter?

_____

4. Which two tables have the same perimeter?

_____

5. You want to put streamers around the edges
of all the tables. How many feet will you need
in all?_____

6. You want to make tablecloths to cover all the tables.
How many square feet of material will you need to cover
all the tables? _____

Pool People

The line graph shows how many people visited the town pool each day.
Use the graph to answer the questions.

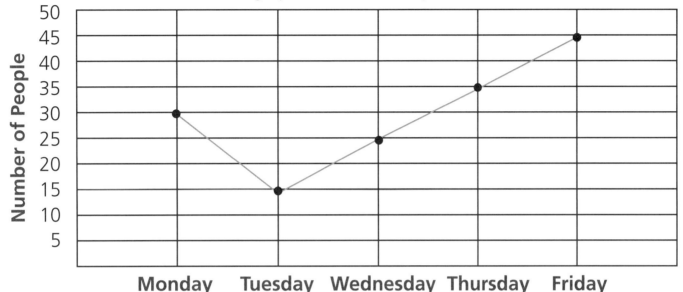

1. Write a number sentence to find how many people visited the pool total from Monday through Friday. _____

2. If *b* equals the number of boys at the pool, write an equation to show how many girls there were at the pool on Tuesday. _____

3. Between which two days did the number of people at the pool decrease by half? _____

4. Write an equation to show the rate of increase from Tuesday through Friday.

   _____

5. Which two days had a combined total of 65 people at the pool?

   _____

6. If the number of people continued to rise at the same rate, how many people would be at the pool on Saturday? _____

Get Set!

Find the mean, the median, and the mode for each set of numbers.

> 3, 7, 1, 6, 3
>
> **Mean**
> Add up all the numbers and divide by how many in the set.
> 3 + 7 + 1 + 6 + 3 = 20
> 20 ÷ 5 = 4
> The mean is 4.
>
> **Median**
> Order the numbers from least to greatest and find the number in the middle.
> 1, 3, 3, 6, 7
> The median is 3.
>
> **Mode**
> Mode is the number that occurs most frequently.
> The mode is 3.

4, 1, 4	3, 10, 2, 4, 5, 2, 2
1. Mean: _____	**4.** Mean: _____
2. Median: _____	**5.** Median: _____
3. Mode: _____	**6.** Mode: _____
2, 5, 4, 2, 2	4, 10, 4, 6
7. Mean: _____	**10.** Mean: _____
8. Median: _____	**11.** Median: _____
9. Mode: _____	**12.** Mode: _____

Above Average

Sometimes the mean of a data set is also called the average. Look at the box next to each game. Find the row whose numbers have that average.
The row can go across, down, or diagonally.

Average: 6

10	2	12
4	7	5
4	3	3

Average: 4

7	8	5
4	2	2
2	6	3

Rainy Days

The graph shows the number of inches of rain that fell each day during the rainstorm.
Use the graph to answer the questions below.

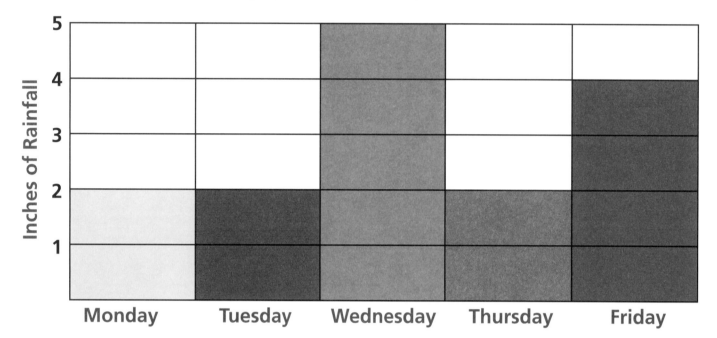

1. Find the average amount of rainfall for the five days. _____

2. How many more inches did it rain on Wednesday than Tuesday?

_____

3. Find the median amount of rainfall for the week. _____

4. How many total inches of rain fell over the five days? _____

5. Find the mode for all the rainfall data. _____

6. Between which two days did the amount of rainfall stay exactly the same?

_____

Will Graph for Laughs

Find each coordinate on the graph and write the letter to answer the joke.

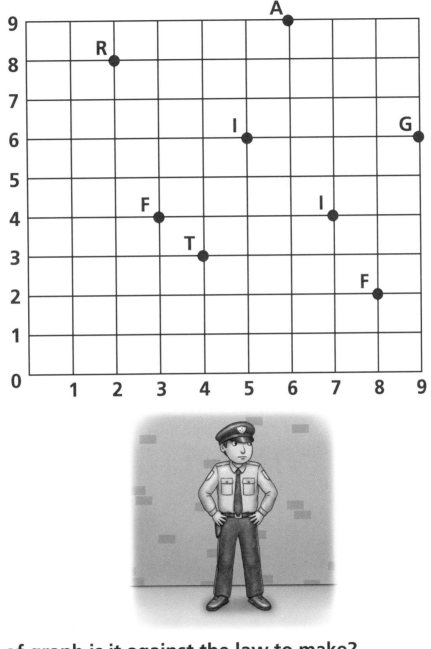

What kind of graph is it against the law to make?

9, 6	2, 8	6, 9	3, 4	8, 2	7, 4	4, 3	5, 6

Grocery Graph

The coordinate graph shows where different foods are located in the grocery store.
Use the graph to answer the questions below.

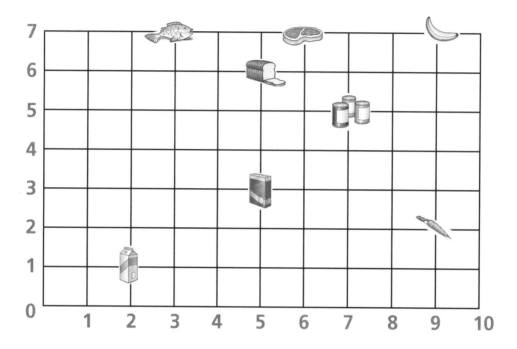

1. Write the coordinates for each food:

milk _____   fish _____

cereal _____   canned food _____

bread _____   meat _____

vegetables _____ fruit _____

2. Pete just put meat in his grocery cart. He needs milk and carrots, too. Which item is closer? _____

3. Circle the two items that look like they are in the same aisle:

   meat   **bread**   **cereal**   **milk**

4. Karen has her cart at the coordinates 3,6. Pete is located at 6,3. Which person is closer to the fish? _____

The Talent Show

The talent show judges gave each performer a score out of 10.
Read each question and find the answer.

1. Kara received three scores of 7, an 8, and a 6 for her dance in the show. What was her average score? _____

2. Russ played the piano for the talent show. The judge's scores were as follows: 8, 7, 8, 8, 7. What is the mode of Russ's scores? _____

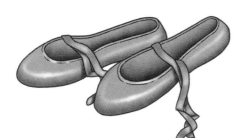

3. After Kelly sang her song, the first two judges gave her a 9. The third judge gave her an 8, and the last two judges both gave her a 7. Find Kelly's median score. _____

4. Did Kara, Russ, or Kelly get the highest score out of 50? _____

Flower Power

Circle the correct answer for each question. Use the picture of the flower bouquet.

1. What are your chances of picking a 🌹 ?

　　a) 2 out of 5　　　　　b) 1 out of 2　　　　　c) 1 out of 10

2. What is the ratio of 🌷 to 🌹 in the bouquet?

　　a) 2:5　　　　　b) 5:2　　　　　c) 2:10

3. Which fraction shows the probability of picking a 🌼 ?

　　a) $\frac{7}{10}$　　　　　b) $\frac{3}{7}$　　　　　c) $\frac{3}{10}$

4. What are the odds you will pick a 🌹 ?

　　a) 50%　　　　　b) 20%　　　　　c) 30%

5. What is the ratio of 🌼 to 🌷 ?

　　a) 2:3　　　　　b) 3:2　　　　　c) 3:10

6. What is the probability you will pick a 🌷 or a 🌹 ?

　　a) 1:2　　　　　b) 5:5　　　　　c) 7:10

Coin Crossword

Use the bag of coins to answer the questions.
Fill the answers into the puzzle.

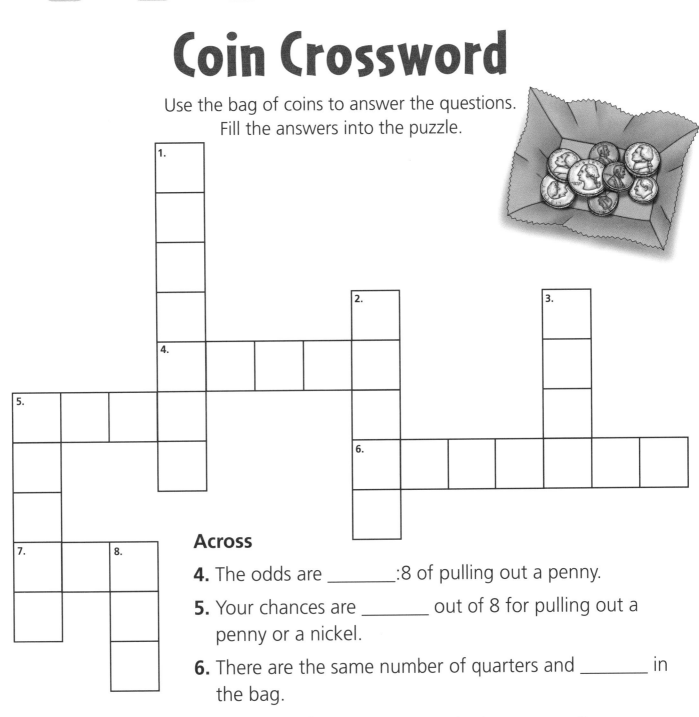

Across

4. The odds are _____:8 of pulling out a penny.

5. Your chances are _____ out of 8 for pulling out a penny or a nickel.

6. There are the same number of quarters and _____ in the bag.

7. The ratio of quarters to pennies is _____: 3.

Down

1. Your chances of pulling this coin out of the bag are one out of four.

2. The odds are 3:8 you will pick this coin.

3. $\frac{1}{8}$ of the coins in the bag are this coin.

5. If you take one of the coins out of the bag and toss it, you have a _____ percent chance of getting heads.

8. _____-fourth of the coins in the bag are nickels.

Pattern Puzzler

Find the rule for each number pattern. Fill in the missing numbers.

1. 5, 10, _____, 20, 25, 30, _____, _____

2. 100, 92, _____, 76, 68, _____, 52, 44

3. _____, 6, 12, 24, _____, 96, 192, _____

4. 3, _____, 33, 48, 63, _____, 93, 108

5. 80, 40, _____, 10, _____, 2.5

6. 18, _____, 30, 36, _____, 48, _____

Find the sequence or rule for each pattern. Fill in the missing letters, numbers, or symbols.

7. X, O, X, O, O, _____, O, _____, _____, O

8. A, C, _____, G, I, _____, M, O

9. 2*x*, 3*x*, _____, 5*x*, 6*x*, _____, _____

10. A, B, C, B, _____, B, C, _____

11.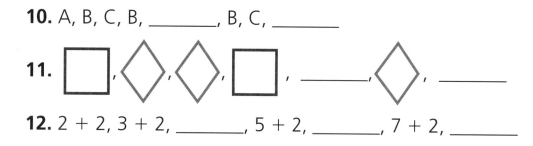

12. 2 + 2, 3 + 2, _____, 5 + 2, _____, 7 + 2, _____

Tricky Transfer

The pictograph shows how many buses are on each route every day.
Use the data from the pictograph to fill in the bar graph below.

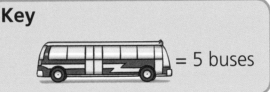

Key

= 5 buses

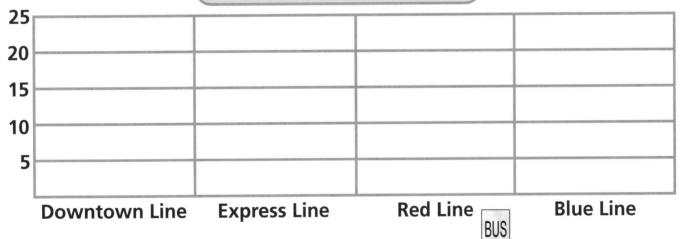

Speedy Sprout

The science class measured a plant's height and counted the number of leaves every three days. Use the data to answer the questions below.

Day	Height	Number of Leaves
1	2 cm	0
4	4 cm	1
7	6 cm	2
10	8 cm	3
13	10 cm	4

1. If the plant continues to grow at the same rate, what will the height be on day 16? _____

2. If the number of leaves continues to increase at the same rate, what day will it be when the plant has 6 leaves?_____

3. The plant grows about how many centimeters every 3 days? _____

4. Assuming the plant grows at the same rate, how tall will it be at the end of the month on day 31? _____

5. If the leaves continue growing at the same rate, how many leaves would the plant have at the end of the month? _____

6. Assuming the height and growth continue at the same rate, how many leaves would the plant have if it was 16 cm tall? _____

The General Store

The General Store is open from 10:00 AM to 5:00 PM. The store owner kept track of the number of customers in the store every hour. Use the graph to figure out if the generalizations below are true or false.

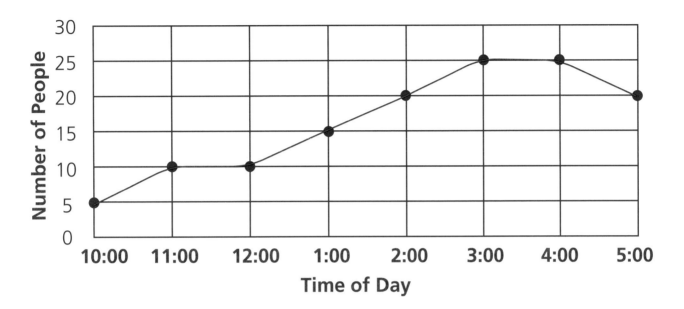

1. The morning hours are busier than the afternoon hours. **true** **false**

2. There are about the same number of customers at opening
and closing time. **true** **false**

3. The number of customers increases later in the day. **true** **false**

4. Late afternoon is the busiest time at the store. **true** **false**

5. Business at the store is slower in the morning. **true** **false**

6. In the middle of the day the number of customers decreases. **true** **false**

Answer Key

Page 4
2. 7
3. 1
4. 5
5. 2
6. 0
7. thousands
8. tens
9. hundred-thousands
10. ones
11. millions
12. ten thousands

Page 5

four thousand, four hundred	4,000 + 400	4,404	40,414
4,000 + 40 + 10 + 14	4,400	4 thousands, 4 hundreds, 4 ones	40,000 + 400 + + 10 + 14
4 thousands, 4 hundreds, 4 tens	fifty-four thousand	2,202 × 2	4 ten-thousands, 4 hundreds, 1 ten, 4 ones
4,414	4 thousands, 4 hundreds, 1 ten, 4 ones	4,000 + 400 + 10 + 4	four thousand, four hundred, fourteen

Page 6
1. 3,600
2. 450,000
3. thousands
4. 790
5. 3,000,000
6. 700
7. 200,000
8. Two (147 and 129)
9. 200
10. 5,410,000
11. hundreds
12. 100

Page 7
1. 204; 240; 402; 2,042; 2,400; 4,002; 4,200
2. 17,560; 17,056; 16,705; 15,760; 10,756; 10,657
3. 328 > 283 > 238 < 382 < 832
4. 1,720 > 1,702 > 1,072 < 1,207 < 1,270
They were gathering counter-intelligence.

Page 8
1. 41.23, 42.13, 42.31, 43.12
2. 517.50, 517.05, 515.70, 515.07
3. >
4. <
5. 54.4
6. 211.6
7. 423.1
8. 66.5
9. 155
10. 32
11. 620
12. 87

Page 9
1. encyclopedias, dictionaries, atlases, almanacs
2. Joyce
3. All three classes round to 200.
4. Clouds and Ocean

Page 10
1. >
2. <
3. 578.23 < 578.32 < 57,832
4. 12.04 < 12.4 > 12 > 1.24
5. 3.46, 34.6, 346
6. 61, 61.05, 61.5
7. 10.02, 10.20, 12, 102
8. 8.09, 80.79, 89, 807.9
9. 92, 9.2, .92
10. 5,108; 580.01; 508.1
11. 4,300.2; 4,230; 4,032; 430.2
12. 1,061.98; 1,061.89; 1,061; 16.01

Page 11
The following numbers should be circled:
2. 7
3. 10
4. 6
5. 6
6. 18
7. 54
8. 38
9. 7
10. 46
At the factory

Page 12
1. 3, 5, 15, 1
2. 3, 9, 1
3. 16, 2, 4, 8, 32, 1
4. 5, 8, 2, 20, 10, 4, 40, 1
5. 18
6. 22
7. 32
8. 48
9. 11
10. 7
11. 3
12. 13

Page 13

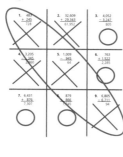

Page 14
2. –3
3. –7
4. –8
5. –9
6. –6
8. –2
9. 0
10. 2
11. –1
12. –3

Page 15
1. –4 degrees
2. 5 degrees
3. 3 dollars
4. –9 degrees

Page 16
1. 589
2. 123
3. 1,999
4. 35,984
5. 3,111
6. 752,470
7. 21,021
8. 415,120
9. 2,103,123
10. 121,899
11. 62,223
12. 738,869

Page 17

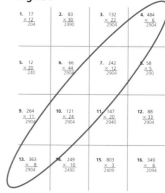

Page 18
2. 5
3. 6
4. 9
5. 1
6. 4
7. 2
8. 7
9. 0
10. 8
11. 5
12. 8

Page 19
1. 2,837
2. 2,014
3. 355
4. 503
5. 223
6. 302
7. 154
8. 250
9. 1,030
10. 1,628
In a school buzz

Page 20
1. 2
2. 4
3. 4
4. 2
5. 13
6. 3
7. 0
8. 14
9. 13
10. 12
11. 5
12. 14

Page 21
1. 1,481 more pizzas
2. 122
3. 100
4. 18 more pizzas were sold on Saturday.

Page 22
1. 8.21
2. 6.55
3. 0.47
4. $242.88
5. 7.54
6. 199
7. $10.98
8. $194.50
9. 0.90
10. 3.01
11. 590.95
12. 27.63

Page 23
Across:
3. 202.39
6. 5.28
8. 878.2
9. 199.7
10. 717.01

Down:
1. 225.52
2. 527.2
4. 288.77
5. 388.72
7. 101.16

Page 24
1. $\frac{2}{8}$ or $\frac{1}{4}$
2. $\frac{3}{5}$
3. $\frac{2}{3}$
4. $\frac{9}{9}$ or 1
5. $\frac{3}{7}$
6. $\frac{1}{10}$
7. $\frac{3}{9}$ or $\frac{1}{3}$
8. $\frac{4}{8}$ or $\frac{1}{2}$
9. $\frac{4}{5}$
10. $\frac{4}{7}$
11. $\frac{6}{10}$ or $\frac{3}{5}$
12. $\frac{2}{5}$

Page 25
2. $\frac{4}{10} - \frac{3}{10} = \frac{1}{10}$
3. $\frac{1}{10} + \frac{4}{10} = \frac{5}{10}$ or $\frac{1}{2}$
4. $\frac{2}{10} + \frac{4}{10} = \frac{6}{10}$ or $\frac{3}{5}$
5. $\frac{3}{10} - \frac{2}{10} = \frac{1}{10}$
6. $\frac{4}{10} - \frac{2}{10} = \frac{2}{10}$ or $\frac{1}{5}$

Page 26
1. 1.95
2. $\frac{4}{8}$ or $\frac{1}{2}$
3. 1.08
4. 20,649
5. $\frac{2}{6}$ or $\frac{1}{3}$
6. 2,327.04
7. $1.74
8. 194.57
9. 119.44
10. 2.91
11. $11.25
12. $\frac{3}{9}$ or $\frac{1}{3}$

Page 27
1. $\frac{3}{8}$
2. $16.25
3. $\frac{5}{6}$
4. No, the pie weighs too much (20.85 ounces).

Page 28
1. They both sold 622 tickets.
2. $108.75
3. 2; grades 2 and 5
4. grade 1
5. 44 (The rounded total is 1,200, and the exact total is 1,244.)
6. $1,555.00

Page 29
1. $\frac{1}{10}$
2. bunny
3. $\frac{7}{10}$
4. dog, cat, bird
5. $\frac{7}{10}$
6. $\frac{6}{10}$ or $\frac{3}{5}$

Page 30
1. 152
2. 1,225
3. 456
4. 927
5. 5,632
6. 6,376
7. 15,012
8. 5,049
9. 63,888
10. 10,528
11. 792
12. 35,200

Page 31

1. 17 ×12 204	2. 83 ×30 2490	3. 132 ×22 2904	4. 484 ×6 2904
5. 12 ×20 240	6. 66 ×44 2904	7. 242 ×12 2904	8. 58 ×5 290
9. 264 ×11 2904	10. 121 ×24 2904	11. 147 ×20 2940	12. 88 ×33 2904
13. 363 ×8 2904	14. 249 ×10 2490	15. 803 ×3 2409	16. 349 ×6 2094

Page 32
1. 375
2. 11,935
3. 5,649
4. 8,208
5. 5,728
6. 24,552
7. 20,975
8. 12,412
9. 21,850
10. 25,235
11. 15,677
12. 34,090

Page 33
2. 52 R4
3. 387 R7
4. 37 R8
5. 48 R5
6. 431 R2
7. 214 R3
8. 189 R6
9. 12 R9
A dandelion

Page 34
1. 347
2. 13
3. 88
4. 582
5. 261
6. 21
7. 783
8. 528
9. 4,074
10. 294
11. 694
12. 156

Page 35
1. 3 bags. There will be 80 pretzels left over.
2. He bought 3 jumbo boxes and 2 small boxes.
3. 94 chocolate chips and 564 peanuts
4. 5 trays (4 trays would make 24, so he needs one more tray to get 28)

Page 36
1. true
2. false (13 and 7 are also factors of 91)
3. false
4. true
5. false
6. true
7. true
8. true
9. true
10. false
11. false (106 is not a multiple of 7)
12. false

Page 37
1. factor tree of 36: 9 and 4; 3, 3 and 2, 2
2. factor tree of 48: 6 and 8; 3, 2 and 4, 2; 2, 2
3. factor tree of 60: 10 and 6; 5, 2 and 3, 2
4. factor tree of 78: 2 and 39; 3 and 13

Page 38
1. $26.32
2. 82.10
3. $3.96
4. $28.74
5. 320.25
6. $31.35
7. $202.50
8. 397.95
9. $27.65
10. $30.55
11. 5,654.4
12. $8.25

Page 39
1. Jared
2. Sara
3. Josh
4. Dawn
5. Lisa
6. Ethan

Page 40
1. 143.64
2. 4.8
3. 8.75
4. 24.13
5. 5,403.71
6. 17.92
7. 5.65
8. 3.5
9. 5,670.2
10. 3,710.76
11. 16.5
12. 2.43

Page 41
1. 17.5 seconds
2. $3.15
3. 65.12 seconds
4. 89 cars

Page 42
1. $\frac{3}{10}$ $\frac{1}{3}$ (crossed out) .3
2. .9 $\frac{9}{10}$ $\frac{9}{09}$ (crossed out)
3. $\frac{1}{5}$ .02 $\frac{2}{10}$
4. $\frac{1}{2}$ $\frac{1}{5}$ (crossed out) .5
5. .25 $\frac{1}{4}$ $\frac{4}{40}$ (crossed out)
6. .75 $\frac{3}{4}$ .34 (crossed out)
7. .1 $\frac{1}{10}$ .01 (crossed out)
8. .5 $\frac{1}{2}$ $\frac{2}{?}$ (crossed out)

Page 43
Grid of fractions (circled answers):
$\frac{2}{3}$	$\frac{6}{9}$	$\frac{4}{12}$
$\frac{3}{15}$	$\frac{5}{15}$	$\frac{6}{24}$
$\frac{8}{24}$	$\frac{7}{21}$	$\frac{5}{20}$
$\frac{5}{10}$	$\frac{5}{35}$	$\frac{6}{12}$
$\frac{1}{5}$	$\frac{3}{21}$	$\frac{8}{16}$
$\frac{5}{25}$	$\frac{4}{20}$	$\frac{8}{40}$

Page 44
2. .04
3. .8
4. .50
5. .01
6. .3
8. $\frac{4}{10}$ or $\frac{2}{5}$
9. $\frac{9}{100}$
10. $\frac{7}{10}$
11. $\frac{3}{100}$
12. $\frac{80}{100}$ or $\frac{4}{5}$

Page 45
T C A B I H R L S G S
.1 $\frac{2}{10}$ .25 .3 $\frac{2}{5}$ $\frac{1}{2}$ .6 $\frac{1}{2}$ .75 $\frac{4}{5}$ $\frac{9}{10}$

Because she had such a bright class

Page 46
2. .19
3. .25
4. .37
5. .4
6. .6
7. $\frac{3}{4}$
8. $\frac{1}{20}$
9. $\frac{21}{100}$
10. $\frac{2}{5}$
11. $\frac{33}{50}$
12. $\frac{9}{100}$

Page 47
1. the package labeled .75 pounds
2. $\frac{5}{100}$ or $\frac{1}{20}$, .05
3. .3
4. fish tacos

Page 48
1. $1\frac{1}{4}$
2. $2\frac{1}{3}$
3. $2\frac{1}{4}$
4. $1\frac{1}{5}$
5. $2\frac{2}{3}$
6. $3\frac{1}{2}$
7. $\frac{3}{2}$
8. $\frac{11}{5}$
9. $\frac{7}{4}$
10. $\frac{13}{5}$
11. $\frac{4}{3}$
12. $\frac{13}{4}$

Page 49
Across:
1. 1.13
3. 1.75
4. 5.75
6. 2.1
7. 2.5
8. 1.2

Down:
1. 1.7
2. 3.25
3. 1.25
5. 5.21

Page 50
2. 6, $\frac{2}{6}$ and $\frac{3}{6}$
3. 8, $\frac{6}{8}$ and $\frac{1}{8}$
4. 20, $\frac{4}{20}$ and $\frac{5}{20}$
5. 24, $\frac{15}{24}$ and $\frac{20}{24}$
6. 15, $\frac{10}{15}$ and $\frac{9}{15}$
7. 12, $\frac{2}{12}$ and $\frac{3}{12}$
8. 9, $\frac{2}{9}$ and $\frac{3}{9}$

Page 51
Flowers with fractions:
$\frac{9}{14}$ $\frac{21}{63}$ $\frac{12}{15}$ $\frac{3}{5}$ $\frac{4}{9}$ $\frac{2}{10}$ $\frac{5}{12}$ $\frac{6}{14}$ $\frac{11}{16}$ $\frac{6}{35}$ $\frac{13}{23}$ $\frac{2}{7}$ $\frac{7}{10}$ $\frac{6}{8}$ $\frac{9}{18}$ $\frac{4}{24}$ $\frac{3}{33}$ $\frac{17}{34}$ $\frac{2}{3}$

$\frac{4}{9}$ $\frac{9}{14}$ $\frac{13}{23}$ $\frac{2}{7}$ $\frac{3}{5}$ $\frac{6}{35}$ $\frac{7}{10}$ $\frac{2}{3}$ $\frac{5}{12}$ $\frac{11}{16}$

Page 52
2. $\frac{1}{8} + \frac{2}{8} = \frac{3}{8}$
3. $\frac{1}{15} + \frac{3}{15} = \frac{4}{15}$
4. $\frac{7}{10} - \frac{2}{10} = \frac{5}{10}$ or $\frac{1}{2}$
5. $\frac{9}{12} + \frac{8}{12} = \frac{17}{12}$ or $1\frac{5}{12}$
6. $\frac{3}{12} - \frac{2}{12} = \frac{1}{12}$
7. $\frac{8}{10} - \frac{5}{10} = \frac{3}{10}$
8. $\frac{11}{12} - \frac{10}{12} = \frac{1}{12}$
9. $\frac{3}{24} + \frac{4}{24} = \frac{7}{24}$
10. $\frac{4}{40} + \frac{15}{40} = \frac{19}{40}$
11. $\frac{15}{18} - \frac{10}{18} = \frac{5}{18}$
12. $\frac{5}{20} + \frac{6}{20} = \frac{11}{20}$

Page 53
1. walnuts, almonds, pecans
2. Yes, there is exactly $\frac{1}{2}$ cup left.
3. 5
4. chicken, pork, turkey, beef

Page 54
1. 30 minutes
2. 1
3. 3
4. 6
5. 225
6. 2 notes each day

Page 55
1. summer
2. 1.5 inches or $1\frac{1}{2}$
3. .5 or $\frac{1}{2}$ inch more
4. winter and summer
5. .4 and $\frac{4}{10}$ or $\frac{2}{5}$
6. 2.1 or $2\frac{1}{10}$

Page 56
1. 9 in.²
2. 8 in.²
3. 15 in.²
4. 16 in.²
5. 6 inches
6. 40 ft.²

Page 57
Grid of shapes (circled answers):
16	12	12
24	16	18
21	12	16

Page 58
1. 6 inches
2. 24 feet
3. 8.5 cm
4. 15 feet
5. 20 inches
6. 28.64 cm
7. 10 inches
8. 6.44 cm
9. 1,012.42 feet

Page 59
2. 75 cm²
3. 11 cm²
4. 126 cm²
5. 40 cm²
6. 125 cm²
A square meal

Page 60
1. cone
2. cube
3. pyramid
4. sphere
5. rectangular prism
6. cylinder

Page 61
1. Westwood Field has a perimeter of 210 feet, and Overland Field has a perimeter of 180 feet. She should jog around Westwood Field to get the longer run.
2. 40 feet
3. 4 times
4. The outdoor court has the larger area of 2,500 square feet, and the indoor court only has an area of 2,400 square feet.

Page 62
1. acute
2. obtuse
3. right
4. acute
5. right
6. obtuse
7. acute
8. acute
9. acute
10. right
11. obtuse
12. obtuse

Page 63
Across | **Down**
1. parallelogram | 2. rhombus
4. isosceles | 3. equilateral
6. cube | 5. square
7. trapezoid
8. scalene

Page 64
1. congruent
2. congruent
3. non-congruent
4. congruent
5. non-congruent
6. non-congruent

Page 65
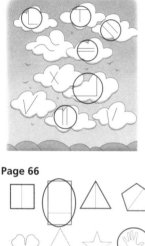

Page 66

Page 67
1. Equilateral triangle

2. Parallel lines

3. Right triangle

4. Rhombus

Page 68
1. 14
2. 67
3. 6
4. 13
5. 13
6. 8
7. 6
8. 32
9. 75
10. 16
11. 2
12. 64

Page 69

$7n$	a number times 7	a number minus 7
$7 - n$	7 less than a number	$n - 7$
a number plus 7	$n + 7$	7 more than a number
$n - 2$	2 more than a number	$2n$
2 less than a number	$2 + n$	twice a number
$n + n$	$2 - n$	$n \times 2$

Page 70
1. 10
2. 7
3. 16
4. 6
5. 5
6. 125
7. 5
8. 25
9. 36
10. 56
11. 10
12. 10

Page 71
2. 3
3. 14
4. 19
5. 23
6. 20
7. 13
8. 7
9. 26
10. 27
A volleyball

Page 72
1. +
2. ÷
3. ×
4. ×
5. −
6. +
7. −
8. ÷
9. +
10. ×
11. +
12. ×

Page 73
1. b
2. a
3. $(30 \times 1.25) - (18 \times 1.75)$
4. 18×6

Page 74
1. true
2. false
3. false
4. true
5. false
6. true
7. true
8. false
9. true
10. false
11. false
12. true

Page 75
Across | **Down**
3. diameter | 1. feet
6. hours | 2. perimeter
8. area | 4. inches
| 5. minutes
| 7. yards

Page 76
1. 19
2. 5
3. 34
4. 14
5. 8
6. 22
7. 4
8. 6
9. 3
10. 7
11. 2
12. 3

Page 77

$4x + y = 12$ — $x= 3, y = 7$
$7x - y = 14$ — $x= 4, y = 16$
$5x + y = 7$ — $x= 5, y = 3$
$3x + 3y = 15$ — $x= 2, y = 4$
$6x - y = 8$ — $x= 1, y = 2$
$2x - 2y = 4$ — $x= 2, y = 3$

Page 78
1. 7
2. 7
3. 34
4. 50
5. 10
6. 18
7. 5
8. 4
9. 10
10. 3
11. 7
12. 2

Page 79
1. 7 and 5
2. 9 and 7
3. 2
4. 2, 3, and 5

Page 80
1. A and B
2. A
3. C
4. B and D
5. 98 feet
6. 134 square feet

Page 81
1. $30 + 15 + 25 + 35 + 45$
2. $15 - b$ = number of girls
3. Monday and Tuesday
4. number of people + 10
5. Monday and Thursday
6. 55

Page 82
1. 3
2. 4
3. 4
4. 4
5. 3
6. 2
7. 3
8. 2
9. 2
10. 6
11. 5 (When there is an even number in the set, find the average of the two numbers in the middle.)
12. 4

Page 83
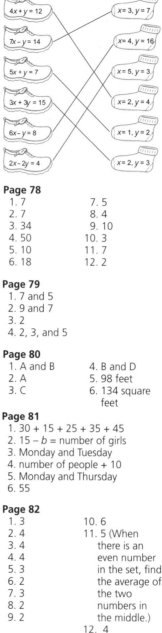

Page 84
1. 3 inches
2. 3 inches more
3. 2 inches
4. 15 inches
5. 2
6. Monday and Tuesday

Page 85
What kind of graph is it against the law to make?

G R A F F I T I
9,6 2,8 6,9 3,4 8,2 7,4 4,3 5,6

Page 86
1. milk 2,1   fish 3,7
   cereal 5,3   canned food 7,5
   bread 5,6   meat 6,7
   vegetables 9,2   fruit 9,7
2. carrots
3. bread and cereal
4. Karen

Page 87
1. 7
2. 8
3. 8
4. Kelly

Page 88
1. b
2. a
3. c
4. a
5. b
6. c

Page 89
Across | **Down**
4. three | 1. quarter
5. five | 2. penny
6. nickels | 3. dime
7. two | 5. fifty
| 8. one

Page 90
1. 15, 35, 40
2. 84, 60
3. 3, 48, 384
4. 18, 78
5. 20, 5
6. 24, 42, 54
7. X, X, O
8. E, K
9. 4x, 7x, 8x
10. A, B
11. ◇ □
12. 2 + 2, 3 + 2, 4 + 2, 5 + 2, 6 + 2, 7 + 2, 8 + 2

Page 91
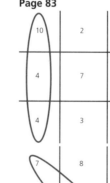

Downtown Line   Express Line   Red Line   Blue Line

Page 92
1. 12 cm
2. Day 19
3. 2 cm
4. 22 cm
5. 10 leaves
6. 7 leaves

Page 93
1. false
2. false
3. true
4. true
5. true
6. false